WINNER'S GUIDE TO GREYHOUND RACING

This book is dedicated to my friend Bob Campbell.

WINNER'S GUIDE TO GREYHOUND RACING

Prof. Jones

Cardoza Publishing

Cardoza Publishing is the foremost gaming publisher in the world with a library of more than 200 up-to-date and easy-to-read books and strategies. These authoritative works are written by the top experts in their fields and with more than 10,000,000 books in print, these books represent the best-selling and most popular gaming books anywhere.

THIRD EDITION
3rd Printing

Copyright © 1993, 1997, 2003 by Prof. Jones
- All Rights Reserved-

Library of Congress Catalog Card No: 2002109182
ISBN: 1-58042-086-9
Author Photo by Clint Broadbent

Visit our web site or write us for a full list of books,
advanced and computer strategies.

CARDOZA PUBLISHING
P.O. Box 98115, Las Vegas, NV 89193
Toll Free Phone (800)577-WINS
email: cardozabooks@aol.com
www.cardozabooks.com

ABOUT THE AUTHOR

Prof. Jones is acknowledged as one of the leading designers of computer software for greyhound, standardbred, thoroughbred, lotto/lottery and sports betting in the world. His very powerful software products are considered to be on the cutting edge of technology by handicappers worldwide. The Prof. Jones software line features more than thirty products on beating the odds. With degrees in Psychology and Statistics, Prof. Jones has always been fascinated with bias and randomness in numbers. He began his handicapping career in 1968, refining his betting skills at the Santa Anita and Hollywood Park race tracks and in 1983, transformed this knowledge into the first computer software that actually produced winners.

Prof. Jones applied his experience and knowledge to create the Pro and Platinum series Greyhound software programs for the everyday player. The basic theories of Prof. Jones' outstanding programs have been simplified and incorporated into the easy-to-read winning strategies presented in this book. For serious greyhound players looking to win more, the acclaimed and successful strategies advertised in the back of the book are highly recommended.

Table of Contents

INTRODUCTION

Greyhound racing has recently become the hottest spectator sport in America. Players that understand how to correctly analyze and bet the dogs are cashing in big on their knowledge. *Winner's Guide to Greyhound Racing* will give you the same knowledge they have so you can play and win like a pro.

Five greyhound strategies are featured in this book for an in-depth analysis of every factor that influences a race. These strategies can be used individually or they can be combined to provide an even more powerful evaluation.

You will learn, step by step, how to accurately determine each dog's class by calculating its Effective Grade, and how best to determine Recent Form, Potential Speed and Running Style. After gaining this insight, you will know how to predict which dogs will be bumped and which will run straight to victory!

You will not only discover how to identify the best dogs,

but also, how to place the most profitable bets. In just a few hours you will be able to win more Trifectas than you ever thought possible; and, with Prof Jones' money management techniques, you will never have to bet more than is necessary.

This book will give you the knowledge and strategy required to consistently identify the best animal or animals. It's packed with a wealth of inside tips and hard-to-find information gathered from successful greyhound handicappers all over the country.

Whether you are a first time enthusiast, or have been handicapping greyhounds for years, read on to become a consistent winner at the track!

WINNING ATTIDUDE

Handicapping, like any other endeavor, requires a conscious effort. Let's study the fundamentals required to be a winning handicapper.

Purchase a Program Early
The first thing that a serious handicapper must do is to purchase the official program. This program is the key to that day's races, and also includes compiled information on such things as kennel standings and track records. The program is about $1.00 and should be purchased no later than the night before the next day's races.

I have been playing every type of race imaginable for the last thirty years and have been associated with many of the world's best handicappers. The old adage among insiders has always been that, "If you have to purchase the program or racing form when you are going through the front door of the track, don't waste your money because it is *too late*."

The best time to purchase the program is the day before the race. You can then allot the uninterrupted time necessary to do an adequate job of handicapping. Think about it. Do you honestly want to invest days or weeks of hard earned money on several minutes of calculations? I doubt that you do, unless betting rather than winning is your only goal.

Set Aside Quality Time

In order to handicap a days races with any degree of accuracy you must be in a quiet environment, with little or no distractions. People who hurriedly grab a program as they are rushing to get their money down on the first race, have no chance. These same "handicappers" then buy a beer and frantically begin circling and underlining past performance lines trying desperately to find a bet, any bet, for the next race.

Set aside quiet time to study the program.

Be a Handicapper, Not a Gambler

Don't laugh at this last statement. Many "gamblers" have

stated that winning is better than losing but playing is all that really counts. They generate a rush of adrenaline when they hear the buzzer go off at the gate and this excites them much more than actually winning.

The professional handicapper will usually only bet several "playable" races each day, whereas, the gambler will bet every race regardless of odds or what the field looks like. In fact, if none of the dogs have ever run at this distance or even at this track, the gambler considers this a better chance for a high payoff and adds more dogs to his Trifecta box.

This book is designed to make you aware of the difference between the handicapper and an ordinary gambler. Anyone can bet money at the track but it takes a determined person to make a consistent profit. This determined person is referred to as a handicapper and this book will give you the tools required to win.

UNDERSTANDING THE RACING PROGRAM

Understanding how to read the racing program is a vital aspect of handicapping. Programs differ from track to track, but contain the same basic information. Although some race data may be in a different order, all programs are essentially alike.

The diagram below shows the typical format for a dog's past performance chart, and points out the items discussed in this book. Each piece of data is noted with a letter and listed in the diagram below.

An explanation of how to read your track's past performances can usually be found in your program. Also, for a complete definition of these items, see this book's Glossary.

A   B   C   D   E

CARL'S WARRIOR   66   (5-2)   Kennel: AAA Racing, Inc.
Red M., March 5, 1990. Blue Rascal - Dana's Lass   Trainer: S.C. Hanson
                                                                              Owner: M. Jones

5-11^{9x}	WL	5-16	F	31.30	65	5	3	4	3	2^1	31.53	4.60	Mvd up after 1/8th	B
5- 8^2	WL	5-16	F	31.38	65	2	4	3	3	3^4	31.69	6.10	Slow start, held on	B
5- 4^3	WL	5-16	F	31.40	64$^{1/2}$	3	2	2	6	4^5	32.36	5.20	Squeezed on rail, ins	B
4-30^3	WL	5-16	F	31.56	65	5	8	6	4	2^1	31.84	9.50	Bumped, strong close	B
4-26^4	WL	5-16	F	31.22	65	6	6	3	3	5^6	32.47	11.00	In trouble twice	B
4-22^3	WL	5-16	F	31.75	66	2	3	3	2	1^1	31.75	8.70	Won driving	C

F G H I   J K L M N O P   Q   R S

A - Name	**K** - Post Weight
B - Current Weight	**L** - Box Position
C - Morning Line Odds	**M** - Start Call
D - Kennel	**N** - 1/8th Call
E - Grade	**O** - Stretch Call
F - Date	**P** - Finish Call
G - Track Time	**Q** - Actual Running
H - Distance	**R** - Odds
I - Track Condition	**S** - Race Comments
J - Winner's Time	

GRADES

Understanding Grades

You must first learn how your track is graded to accurately determine whether a dog is moving up or down in class. **Grading rules** are designed and regulated by each state and track. The following page shows a typical example of the grading rules for a normal Greyhound race track. These rules will differ from track to track and state to state, but are all essentially the same.

As you can see by the grading rules, dogs move up and down in grade due to age and ability. Young dogs must start out in the schooling and maiden ranks, but can quickly move up in grade if they demonstrate the ability to win. Let's now examine the different types of grades and learn which ones provide the best opportunity to make a profit.

Schooling Races

The first races that young pups run are called **schooling races**. Schooling races can easily be identified because there are never any odds in the odds column and there's a dash in the grade column.

These races prepare the dogs for competition and also show the trainers which animals are faster. Considering the fact that there are no wagers on schooling races, I will not elaborate on how to handicap them. The only thing you must remember is that schooling races do not reflect a dog's true abilities. This is because they do not always include eight dogs and often the dogs running are not very disciplined, or do not give a good effort.

A dog might also be forced to run a schooling race later in it's career because it tried to fight in a race, was injured, or recently put in a series of very poor performances and the kennel wants to see it improve.

Regardless of the dog's performance in the schooling race, that race must not be used to approximate how the dog might run in its next race.

In Figure 3.1, notice that King Vic (a dog with an established grade) ran well in his schooling race on 1/29. Based on that schooling race the crowd bet him down to 3-1 in his next race and he ran 5th.

KING VIC									59	(6	Kennel: AAA Racing, Inc. Trainer: S.C. Hanson Owner: M. Jones			
2-11^7	5-16	F	31.85	59	5	6	2	2	3^1	31.92	7.60	Trouble, beat place	C
2- 6^7	5-16	F	31.93	59	8	5	2	1^2	2^1	31.97	6.40	Overtaken stretch	B
2- 2^6	5-16	F	31.65	58 $^{1/2}$ 4	5	4	4	5^4	31.97	2.90	Never contender	B
1-29^{9x}	5-16	F	31.54	59	2	3	1$^{1/2}$	1^1	1^1	31.54	---	Increased lead	-
1-25^8	5-16	F	31.89	60	1	4	6	7	7^8	32.49	4.50	Bumped twice	B
1-20^7	5-16	F	31.68	60 $^{1/2}$ 2	3	3	3	5^5	32.04	4.60	Contended to stretch	B

Figure 3.1–Greyhound Exhibiting a Schooling Race

Typical Grading Rules

There will be five grades for experienced greyhounds. When designating the grades of races the letters A, B, C, D, E, S and M will be used. Grade A shall be the highest classification and Grade E shall be the lowest classification. Grade S indicates special and stakes races. Grade M refers to maiden classification, and indicates greyhounds that have not won an official race.

At any time within a greyhound's first three starts, the Racing Secretary may reclassify the greyhound, but not more than one grade, either to a higher or lower grade. From this classification the grading system will apply in the established manner.

The winner of any grade race shall advance one (1) grade until reaching Grade A.

When a greyhound wins a maiden race, it may be placed no higher than Grade D by the Racing Secretary. Six consecutive starts as a maiden without finishing 4th or better will eliminate that dog from further use.

In lowering a greyhound there are three separate and distinct ways this may be accomplished. By failing to finish 1st, 2nd, or 3rd in three consecutive starts in the same grade; by failing to earn more than one 3rd in four consecutive starts in the same grade; or by failing to earn the equivalent of a win purse in six consecutive starts, this being figured on the basis of six points for first, three points for second, and one point for third.

Exceptions
To be lowered from Grade D to Grade E, a greyhound must fail to finish 1st, 2nd, 3rd or 4th in four consecutive starts. A greyhound that fails to finish 1st, 2nd, 3rd, or 4th in four consecutive starts in Grade E will be eliminated from further use. Falling lines and met interference lines will not count in the fourth start in lowering a greyhound from Grade D to Grade E or in eliminating a greyhound from further use.

The Racing Secretary may select from greyhounds of the same grade to fill feature races twice each week and these races will be designated as Grade S. Entries for all races will be drawn by lot.

All stake and sweepstakes races shall be indicated by the letter "S".

The Racing Secretary may use greyhounds of no more than two different grades for races longer than the Arkansas course and these races shall be designated by the letter "T". Each greyhound in such a race shall have its proper grade indicated in the program.

Greyhounds not racing on account of illness or injury for thirty (30) or more days may be reclassified.

These rules can be different depending on the State Racing Secretary and from year to year.

This example illustrates why schooling races cannot be used to determine how a dog might run in a maiden or graded race.

Maiden Races (M)

After a dog is schooled, it begins racing against other non-winners in **maiden races**. From a wagering standpoint, the field's lack of experience and inconsistency make maiden races a poor bet at best.

The number one reason gamblers (not handicappers) play maidens is because they are unable to pass up a race. Even though there may be less than two previous races per animal, and those are schooling or maiden races, gamblers still feel that they can somehow select the winners.

JERRY'S JET											69	(3-2)	Kennel: AAA Racing, Inc. Trainer: S.C. Hanson Owner: M. Jones
8-13^{11s}	5-16	F	30.96	70	4	5	3	2	1^3	30.96	---	Drew off stretch-in	
8- 9^{7s}	5-16	F	30.71	70	6	4^1	3	2	2^3	30.71	---	Bumped 1st, raced up-in	

Figure 3.2–Greyhound with only two Schooling Races

Other maiden race players study the expert's picks located on the bottom of the program. How can anyone, even the so-called local expert, predict the top four finishers of a maiden race?

8-21$^{...}$	5-16	F	30.53	68	6	5	3	2	2^1	30.57	4.00	Wd trns, chllnged-md	M
8-15^7	5-16	F	30.22	68	6	8	8	6	4^7	30.74	12.70	Early trffc, rallied	M
8-10^{10}	5-16	F	30.06	68	1	6	7	6	5^8	---	15.30	Wd 1s shuffled-in	---
8- 4^7	5-16	F	30.30	69	7	5	7	7	6^3	---	12.00	Never prominent	---

Morning Line 2-4-1-6 TRIFECTA, QUINELLA AND EXACTA WAGERING ON THIS RACE
SECOND HALF QUINELLA DOUBLE

Figure 3.3–Morning Line Favorites

Prior to maiden races, a favorite will actually emerge out of this handicapper's nightmare. The crowd will begin to truly believe that this dog "should win the race." Thirty seconds later a lot of people are disappointed and can't understand why the favorite lost. Do not get caught up in this "mass hysteria." Since there is not enough information, never bet maiden races under any circumstances.

Maiden Winners

After a dog wins its first race, it is no longer considered a maiden. Normally the dog goes into the next higher grade (D), although some tracks allow dogs to go as high as C grade after their first win. The betting public often becomes confused about the ability of recent maiden winners.

LITTLE BLAZE 63 (4) Kennel: AAA Racing, Inc.
Trainer: S.C. Hanson
Owner: M. Jones

2-26^3	5-16	F	31.64	63	6	4	2	1^3	1^5	31.64	3.10	Despite trouble at1st	M
2+22^2	5-16	F	31.68	62	4	3	2	2	2^2	31.95	4.50	Good early effort to plc	M
2+19^9	5-16	F	32.10	63	5	5	3	4	3^3	32.33	7.30	Good fin effort-md	M
1+14^4	5-16	F	31.09	63	5	3	5	7	6^7	32.19	---	Collided entrg bkstr	
2- 8^1	5-16	F	31.71	63	7	1^{12}	2^1	2^2	2^1	31.82	---	Hard try, inside	

Figure 3.4–Recent Maiden Winner

Whether it was a very fast speed, or a five-length win, these maiden winners often go off as favorites in their next race. The crowd somehow completely forgets that the dog will now be running against much more experienced animals.

Optimistic bettors believe that the maiden winner will continue to win each race. They feel (or hope) that this is really a young A grade dog racing in D or C grade company. Unfortunately, most dogs never see the A grades and many never even rise above the D or C grade that they achieved after winning their maiden race.

SALLY SIOUX 53 (7-2)

Kennel: AAA Racing, Inc.
Trainer: S.C. Hanson
Owner: M. Jones

6

7-30[7]	5-16	F	32.05	52	8	6	4	4	6[6]	31.92	7.60	Much trouble	D
7-26[7]	5-16	F	31.81	53	6	1[1]	1[1ª] 2	4[6]	31.97	10.20	Set early pace	D
7-21[6]	5-16	F	31.87	53	5	4	8	8	8	31.97	5.60	Pulled up	D
7-17[9x]	5-16	F	31.73	52	4	1	8	6	5[9]	31.54	3.50	No factor	D
7-12[8]	5-16	F	31.78	53	8	5	1[1]	1[2] 1[5]	32.49	5.40	Pulling away	M
7- 8[7]	5-16	F	32.25	52	3	7	7	5	4[2]	32.04	5.80	Bumped 1st turn	M

Figure 3.5–Probable Lower-Grade Greyhound

It must be assumed that a maiden winner is not only going up in class after its maiden win, but realistically, is now racing in uncharted territory against tougher and more seasoned animals. Its fast times or lengths ahead at the finish in its maiden win must be tempered with the harsh reality that this dog is now making a major move up in class and has a good chance of losing. For these reasons, do not bet maiden winners in their next race.

Lowest Grade Races (D & E)

Another big drawback to playing maiden winners is the type of dogs that they will be racing against at the lower grades. These young winners will face older A or B grade animals that are at the end of their career, along with other maiden winners that are destined for A grade. They will also be running against a large group of perennial low grade contenders that occasionally win if the conditions are right.

Interestingly enough, even with the diversity of dogs in these races, more false favorites occur at lower grades than any other. As you might have guessed after reading the last section, these false favorites are most often maiden winners running their first race. Fans get excited about the possibilities of these pups and have a tendency to make them favorites, normally false favorites.

You must never bet maiden races, and also never bet lower grade races. They contain too many dogs starting and ending careers.

Middle and Higher Grade Races (B & C)

The **second** and **third grades** from the top, normally **B** and **C**, make the most lucrative bets at any track. These dogs are not only consistent, but you can also easily identify which dogs are dropping or rising in class. The strongest animals are the ones that have won at a higher grade, but are temporarily out of form and have been forced to drop in class.

In order to decide which dogs are actually dropping in class, you must review older racing programs and analyze at least the last twelve races. If today was a C grade race, the greyhound in Figure 3.6 would be a likely class contender.

3

| MILO'S THUNDER | | | | | | | | | | | | | | **79** | **(9-2)** | Kennel: AAA Racing, Inc. Trainer: S.C. Hanson Owner: M. Jones |

7-	4^{12}	5-16	F	30.50	80^{12}	2	3	2	2	2^1	30.51	2.50	Held strong place-in	C
6-30	30^2	5-16	F	30.50	79	8	6	5	6	4^5	30.55	3.20	Crowded bk 1st-in	C
6-25	25^{10x}	5-16	F	30.59	79	7	5	5	5	6^7	30.67	6.30	No mishaps on-rl	C
6-20	20^2	5-16	F	30.69	78	3	6	6	7	5^{412}	30.74	4.50	Cowded bk 2nd-in	B
6-16	16^7	5-16	F	30.57	78^{12}	1	4	2	4	4^2	30.72	6.80	Followed leaders-in	B
6-11	11^{8x}	5-16	F	30.51	79	6	3	3	5	8^6	30.69	7.00	Trffc 1st, bmpd-md	B
6-	7^3	5-16	F	30.52	80	2	2	1^1	1^2	1^2	30.52	2.10	Withstood pressure-in	C
6-	2^4	5-16	F	30.55	78	6	5	4	4	5^4	30.63	5.60	Never prominent-md	B
5-29	29^7	5-16	F	30.71	79	8	8	7	7	6^6	30.80	8.40	Wd 1st, held showin	B
5-25	25^{10}	5-16	F	30.60	79	1	3	3	3	4^{312}	30.65	11.40	Collided 2nd-md	B
5-20	20^7	5-16	F	30.50	78	5	3	1	5	6^5	30.57	6.70	Squeezed bk str-in	A
5-16	16^8	5-16	F	30.54	78	2	2	3	4	4^3	30.56	9.20	Drifted back-in	A

Figure 3.6–Higher Grade Greyhound in Lower Grade Race

According to the last twelve races, this dog recently failed at A and B grades but should prove very strong against the C grade dogs it will be facing today.

Highest Grade Races (A)

Grade A races are almost as difficult to beat as D grade and lower because the dogs are so evenly matched. Another problem is that you never have any dogs dropping in class because A is the highest possible grade.

If you do decide to play A grade races, look for dogs that are consistent A grade winners and have been at that grade for at least six races. These animals are a better bet than B grade winners that have just graduated to A grade. The only exception to this might be a young B grade winner that appears to be moving up fast and is running against slightly less consistent A grade animals.

Determining a Dog's Effective Grade

Determining each animal's class or effective grade is probably the most important element in greyhound handicapping. If a dog has more class than the animals if faces, it is usually a strong contender.

The average player studies the program in order to determine each dog's grade. Using the last 6 races, which is only about one month of a dog's life, they try very hard to figure out which dog or dogs have the most class. As was previously noted, it is difficult to make an accurate grade determination using just the last 6 races. This will become apparent in the following example.

Below is what today's program might look like for a typical dog running a C grade race. An appraisal of its grade is almost impossible using only the last six races.

5

SHOOTING ASTRO   **62**   **(8)**   Kennel: AAA Racing, Inc.
                                                                    Trainer: S.C. Hanson
                                                                    Owner: M. Jones

8-31^1	5-16	F	30.27	61	4	3	4	3	3^4	31.69	4.30	Never prominent-in	C
8-27^2	5-16	F	30.78	61	4	4	3	4	4^3	31.53	3.70	Never challenged	B
8-21^{12x}	5-16	F	30.53	61	2	2	2	3	6^9	32.07	5.80	Fell stretch, tired	B
8-15^{12}	5-16	F	30.67	60	1	1^1	4	5	4^5	31.82	8.50	Bumped wd 1st	B
8-10^{8x}	5-16	F	30.53	60	4	5	6	4	6^8	31.94	7.10	Never prominent	B
8- 4^{12}	5-16	F	30.34	61	8	8	7	7	2^1	30.66	9.20	Drove up to place	B

Figure 3.7–Determining Grade with 6 Previous Races

Let's now analyze its last twelve races and see if its actual grade is easier to determine.

5

SHOOTING ASTRO															62	(8)		Kennel: AAA Racing, Inc. Trainer: S.C. Hanson Owner: M. Jones

8-31^1	5-16	F	30.27	61	4	3	4	3	3^4	31.69	4.30	Never prominent-in	C
8-27^2	5-16	F	30.78	61	4	4	3	4	4^3	31.53	3.70	Never challenged	B
8-21^{12x}	5-16	F	30.53	61	2	2	2	3	6^9	32.07	5.80	Fell stretch, tired	B
8-15^{12}	5-16	F	30.67	60	1	1^1	4	5	4^5	31.82	8.50	Bumped wd 1st	B
8-10^{8x}	5-16	F	30.53	60	4	5	6	4	6^8	31.94	7.10	Never prominent	B
8- 4^{12}	5-16	F	30.34	61	8	8	7	7	2^1	30.66	9.20	Drove up to place	B
7-31^3	5-16	F	30.78	60	2	2	2	2	3^2	30.98	4.60	No match for W,P	B
7-26^4	5-16	F	30.13	61	8	7	4	4	5^4	31.35	7.30	Stdy gain from outside	A
7-20^6	5-16	F	30.22	61	8	8	7	7	7^9	31.74	8.00	Never prominent	A
7-15^2	5-16	F	30.06	60	3	2	4	6	6^7	31.61	5.90	Bmpd wd 1/8th	A
7- 9^3	5-16	F	30.30	61	3	3	4	4	4^3	30.97	3.50	Crowded inside	A
7- 4^5	5-16	F	30.29	61	3	2	2	2	1^1	30.29	2.60	Determined str-in	B

Figure 3.8–Determining Grade with twelve Previous Races

With this additional information it becomes apparent that this is a competitive B grade dog recently running out of form. When back in form, it should easily beat C grade animals. The 6 additional race lines allow a clearer picture of this animal's history and its actual or effective grade.

The effective grade is the grade at which the dog has demonstrated the ability to compete. Let's now look at a similar dog that recently dropped from B grade and also posted a third place finish in C grade last out.

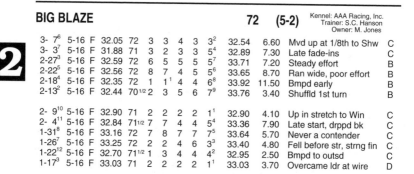

BIG BLAZE   72   (5-2)   Kennel: AAA Racing, Inc. / Trainer: S.C. Hanson / Owner: M. Jones

3-	7^6	5-16	F	32.05	72	3	3	4	3	3^2	32.54	6.60	Mvd up at 1/8th to Shw	C
3-	3^7	5-16	F	31.88	71	3	2	3	3	5^4	32.89	7.30	Late fade-ins	C
2-27	^{3}	5-16	F	32.59	72	6	5	5	5	5^7	33.71	7.20	Steady effort	B
2-22	^{5}	5-16	F	32.56	72	8	7	4	5	5^6	33.65	8.70	Ran wide, poor effort	B
2-18	^{4}	5-16	F	32.35	72	1	1^1	4	4	6^8	33.92	11.50	Bmpd early	B
2-13	^{2}	5-16	F	32.44	70½	2	3	5	6	7^9	33.76	3.40	Shuffld 1st turn	B
2-	9^{10}	5-16	F	32.90	71	2	2	2	2	1^1	32.90	4.10	Up in stretch to Win	C
2-	4^{11}	5-16	F	32.84	71½	7	7	4	4	5^4	33.36	7.90	Late start, drppd bk	C
1-31	^{8}	5-16	F	33.16	72	7	8	7	7	7^5	33.64	5.70	Never a contender	C
1-26	^{7}	5-16	F	33.25	72	2	2	4	6	3^3	33.40	4.80	Fell before str, strng fin	C
1-22	^{12}	5-16	F	32.70	71½	1	3	4	4	4^2	32.95	2.50	Bmpd to outsd	C
1-17	^{3}	5-16	F	33.03	71	2	2	2	2	1^1	33.03	3.70	Overcame ldr at wire	D

Figure 3.9–Greyhound Exhibiting a False Drop in Class

Unlike the previous animal, this dog has been competing with much lower grade dogs. Even though it recently ran four B grade races, it is probably not an effective B grade contender. Both dogs look similar on today's program, but after analyzing the last twelve races, the first animal has a distinct class edge.

In the next section you will learn how to quickly calculate each dogs' effective grade in order to easily identify dogs with a class advantage.

How to Calculate Effective Grade

Even though dogs move up a grade when they win, and drop a grade when they are out of form, they tend to gravitate toward the grade that they show the most consistency. This is the highest grade that they are competitive at, and is referred to as their **effective grade**. If they are currently running at a lower grade than their effective grade and are coming back into form, they make the best bets.

Highlight Grades

The first step in finding the effective grade is to highlight each grade where a dog finished in the top three (1st, 2nd, or 3rd) in its last twelve races. (Always save your programs so you will have the last twelve races.)

In the example below you can see that this dog finished 1st, 2nd or 3rd four times in its last twelve races. The grade it was running when it **lit the board** is highlighted.

4

BONA-FIDO										**66**	**(4-3)**	Kennel: AAA Racing, Inc. Trainer: S.C. Hanson Owner: M. Jones	
6- 9^{9x}	5-16	F	31.30	65	3	3	4	3	3^2	31.86	6.60	Mvd up at 1/8th to Shw	C
6- 4^2	5-16	F	31.38	65	3	4	3	4	4^4	32.14	7.30	Late fade-ins	B
5-31^3	5-16	F	31.40	$64^{1/2}$	6	2	2	3	6^7	32.73	7.20	Outrun at finish	B
5-26^3	5-16	F	31.24	65	8	1	4	5	2^2	31.59	8.70	Erratic outside	B
5-22^4	5-16	F	31.22	65	1	5^1	6	4	6^8	32.42	11.50	Ran wide, poor effort	B
5-17^3	5-16	F	31.18	66	2	8	7	7	7^9	32.93	3.40	Pinnd agnst rail 1st trn	B
5-13^4	5-16	F	31.64	$65^{1/2}$	2	2	2	2	2^1	31.81	4.10	Steady effort	B
5- 8^1	5-16	F	31.50	65	7	7	4	4	5^4	32.06	7.90	Late start, drppd bk	A
5- 4^1	5-16	F	31.06	66	7	8	7	7	7^6	32.11	5.70	Never a contender	A
4-31^2	5-16	F	31.08	$65^{1/2}$	2	2	4	6	3^2	31.20	4.80	Fell before str, strng fin	A
4-27^2	5-16	F	31.47	65.	1	3	4	4	4^2	31.65	2.50	Bmpd to outsd	A
4-23^5	5-16	F	31.53	65	2	2	2	2	1^1	31.53	3.70	Overcame ldr at wire	B

Figure 3.10–Noting Grades in Win, Place, or Show Races

Finding the Grade Score

When you have completed highlighting the grades, use the chart below to decide how many points each top finish receives. (If your track uses AA or any other symbol for the highest grade, give it 5 points, the next grade 4 points, and so on.)

<u>Grade Point Chart</u>

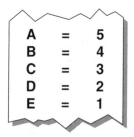

$$A = 5$$
$$B = 4$$
$$C = 3$$
$$D = 2$$
$$E = 1$$

Then place the grade point score to the right of all highlighted grades.

4

BONA-FIDO   66   (4-3)   Kennel: AAA Racing, Inc. / Trainer: S.C. Hanson / Owner: M. Jones

6- 9^{9x}	5-16	F	31.30	65	3	3	4	3	3^2	31.86	6.60	Mvd up at 1/8th to Shw	C
6- 4^2	5-16	F	31.38	65	3	4	3	4	4^4	32.14	7.30	Late fade-ins	B
5-31^3	5-16	F	31.40	64$^{1/2}$	6	2	2	3	6^7	32.73	7.20	Outrun at finish	B
5-26^3	5-16	F	31.24	65	8	1	4	5	2^2	31.59	8.70	Erratic outside	B
5-22^4	5-16	F	31.22	65	1	5^1	6	4	6^8	32.42	11.50	Ran wide, poor effort	B
5-17^3	5-16	F	31.18	66	2	8	7	7	7^9	32.93	3.40	Pinnd agnst rail 1st trn	B
5-13^4	5-16	F	31.64	65$^{1/2}$	2	2	2	2	2^1	31.81	4.10	Steady effort	B
5- 8^1	5-16	F	31.50	65	7	7	4	4	5^4	32.06	7.90	Late start, drppd bk	A
5- 4^1	5-16	F	31.06	66	7	8	7	7	7^6	32.11	5.70	Never a contender	A
4-31^2	5-16	F	31.08	65$^{1/2}$	2	2	4	6	3^2	31.20	4.80	Fell before str, strng fin	A
4-27^2	5-16	F	31.47	65.	1	3	4	4	4^2	31.65	2.50	Bmpd to outsd	A
4-23^5	5-16	F	31.53	65	2	2	2	2	1^1	31.53	3.70	Overcame ldr at wire	B

– 3

– 4

– 4

– 4

Figure 3.11–Calculating a Greyhound's Grade Point

Now add up the total points and divide by the total number of grades that you highlighted (in this example it was four).

$$
\begin{array}{l}
C = 3 \\
B = 4 \\
B = 4 \\
+\ \underline{B = 4} \\
15
\end{array}
$$
    15 divided by 4 = 3.75

This will give you the dog's **grade point score**. You must now match it with the effective grade.

Finding the Effective Grade
Using the chart below, you will be able to determine the effective grade of each dog in the race.

Effective Grade Chart			
Average Points			**Effective Grade**
4.75	to	5.00	A
4.50	to	4.74	A-
4.10	to	4.40	B+
3.75	to	4.00	B
3.50	to	3.74	B-
3.10	to	3.40	C+
2.75	to	3.00	C
2.5	to	2.74	C-
2.10	to	2.40	D+
1.75	to	2.00	D
1.50	to	1.74	D-
1.10	to	1.40	E+
.75	to	1.00	E
.5	to	.74	E-

In the last example, Bona Fido had a grade score of 3.75. According to the chart, this dog has an effective grade of B.

Examples of Determining Effective Grade
For practice, let's evaluate the effective grade of two dogs running at C grade that have different grade histories. This will allow you to see how an **effective**

grade analysis, compared with today's grade, isolates the contenders. Begin by highlighting the grades of all races that Bona-Fido finished in the top three.

BONA-FIDO   **66**   **(4-3)**   Kennel: AAA Racing, Inc.
                                                                        Trainer: S.C. Hanson
                                                                        Owner: M. Jones

6- 9^{9x}	5-16	F	31.30	65	3	3	4	3	3^2	31.86	6.60	Mvd up at 1/8th to Shw	C
6- 4^2	5-16	F	31.38	65	3	4	3	4	4^4	32.14	7.30	Late fade-ins	C
5-31^3	5-16	F	31.40	$64^{1/2}$	6	2	2	3	6^7	32.73	7.20	Outrun at finish	B
5-26^3	5-16	F	31.24	65	8	1	4	5	2^2	31.59	8.70	Erratic outside	B
5-22^4	5-16	F	31.22	65	1	5^1	6	4	6^8	32.42	11.50	Ran wide, poor effort	B
5-17^3	5-16	F	31.18	66	2	8	7	7	7^9	32.93	3.40	Pinnd agnst rail 1st trn	B
5-13^4	5-16	F	31.64	$65^{1/2}$	2	2	2	2	2^1	31.81	4.10	Steady effort	B
5- 8^1	5-16	F	31.50	65	7	7	4	4	5^4	32.06	7.90	Late start, drppd bk	A
5- 4^1	5-16	F	31.06	66	7	8	7	7	7^6	32.11	5.70	Never a contender	A
4-31^2	5-16	F	31.08	$65^{1/2}$	2	2	4	6	6^2	31.20	4.80	Fell before str, strng fin	A
4-27^2	5-16	F	31.47	65.	1	3	4	4	4^2	31.65	2.50	Bmpd to outsd	A
4-23^5	5-16	F	31.53	65	2	2	2	2	1^1	31.53	3.70	Overcame ldr at wire	B

Figure 3.12–Determining Effective Grade

Next add up each grade score, as we did before, and divide by the number of grades used.

$$C=3$$
$$B=4$$
$$B=4$$
$$+ \underline{B=4}$$
$$15$$

15 divided by 4 = 3.75

Finally, compare the dog's effective grade score to the effective grade chart. Bona Fido's effective grade is a 3.75, making it a B grade contender.

4.10	to	**4.40**	**B+**
3.75	to	**4.00**	**B**
3.50	to	**3.74**	**B-**
3.10	to	**3.40**	**C+**

Let's now look at our second example.

8

	CFU CAN										66	(4-3)	Kennel: AAA Racing, Inc. Trainer: S.C. Hanson Owner: M. Jones	

6- 9^{9x}	5-16	F	31.30	65	3	3	4	3	3^2	31.86	6.60	Mvd up at 1/8th to Shw	C
6- 4^2	5-16	F	31.38	65	3	4	3	4	4^4	32.14	7.30	Late fade-ins	C
5-31^3	5-16	F	31.40	64$^{1/2}$	6	2	2	3	6^7	32.73	7.20	Outrun at finish	B
5-26^3	5-16	F	31.24	65	8	1	4	5	2^2	31.59	8.70	Erratic outside	B
5-22^4	5-16	F	31.22	65	5	5^1	6	4	6^8	32.42	11.50	Ran wide, poor effort	B
5-17^3	5-16	F	31.18	66	6	8	7	7	7^9	32.93	3.40	Pinnd agnst rail 1st trn	B
5-13^4	5-16	F	31.64	65$^{1/2}$	2	2	2	2	1^1	31.64	4.10	Steady effort	C
5- 8^1	5-16	F	31.50	65	7	7	4	4	5^4	32.06	7.90	Late start, drppd bk	C
5- 4^1	5-16	F	31.06	66	7	8	7	7	7^6	32.11	5.70	Never a contender	C
4-31^2	5-16	F	31.08	65$^{1/2}$	2	2	4	6	3^2	31.20	4.80	Fell before str, strng fin	C
4-27^2	5-16	F	31.47	65.	1	3	4	4	4^2	31.65	2.50	Bmpd to outsd	C
4-23^5	5-16	F	31.53	65	2	2	2	2	1^1	31.53	3.70	Overcame ldr at wire	D

Figure 3.13–Determining Effective Grade for a Second Greyhound

CFU CAN has top finishes in both D and B grades, along with three finishes in C. Again let's add up the scores and divide the total by the number of grades highlighted to determine the dog's grade score.

$$
\begin{array}{r}
B=4 \\
C=3 \\
C=3 \\
C=3 \\
+\ \underline{D=1} \\
14
\end{array}
$$

14 divided by 5 = 2.80

This animal achieved an average score of 2.80. When you match this to the grade chart the effective grade is C.

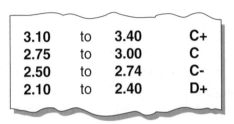

3.10	to	3.40	C+
2.75	to	3.00	C
2.50	to	2.74	C-
2.10	to	2.40	D+

Considering the fact that both of these animals had four B grade races on today's program, but their effective grades were B and C, it is obvious that the dog with an effective grade of B will have the advantage. Without knowing the effective grade, class distinction between dogs is impossible.

Marking Your Program
The final thing is to mark each dogs' effective grade next to its past grades. You will need this information in order to handicap a race.

4

BONA-FIDO   **66**   **(4-3)**   Kennel: AAA Racing, Inc.
Trainer: S.C. Hanson
Owner: M. Jones

6- 9^{9x}	5-16	F	31.30	65	3	3	4	3	3^2	31.86	6.60	Mvd up at 1/8th to Shw	C
6- 4^2	5-16	F	31.38	65	3	4	3	4	4^4	32.14	7.30	Late fade-ins	C
5-31^3	5-16	F	31.40	64½	6	2	2	3	6^7	32.73	7.20	Outrun at finish	B
5-26^3	5-16	F	31.24	65	8	1	4	5	2^2	31.59	8.70	Erratic outside	B
5-22^4	5-16	F	31.22	65	1	5^1	6	4	6^8	32.42	11.50	Ran wide, poor effort	B
5-17^3	5-16	F	31.18	66	2	8	7	7	7^9	32.93	3.40	Pinnd agnst rail 1st trn	B

B

Figure 3.14–Noting the Effective Grade on your Racing Program

ADVANCED GRADE STRATEGY

First Race at Higher Grade

It is a fact that dogs moving up to a grade that they have never run at before win only 15% of the time. Their odds also tend to be low because the public often overreacts to their recent win and also to the fact that they are currently in good form. Figure 3.15 represents a dog that ran its first B grade race.

3

													Kennel: AAA Racing, Inc.
MAX'S DINGO										**76**	**(6)**		Trainer: S.C. Hanson Owner: M. Jones
7- 4^{9x}	5-16	F	30.76	75	3	3	4	4	6^4	31.64	1.30	Outran by field, outsd	B
6-30^{12}	5-16	F	30.76	75	2	2	1	2	1^2	30.76	3.50	Good surges to win	C
6-25^1	5-16	F	30.30	75½	2	2	2	3	3^3	30.82	6.70	Slowed near fin-ins	C
6-21^{1x}	5-16	F	30.65	76	2	1	4	5	5^4	31.29	2.20	Bumped wd, ran far	C
6-17^1	5-16	F	30.40	76	1	1^1	2	2	2^1	30.70	7.60	Ran outsde winner	C
6-12^1	5-16	F	30.66	76	8	8	7	5	3^5	30.93	9.80	Gained in stretch	C
6- 8^{1x}	5-16	F	30.50	75	3	3	4	4	6^5	31.22	6.30	Boxed in at stretch	C
6- 3^{1x}	5-16	F	30.57	76	3	2	4	6	8^9	31.36	1.50	Bumped 1/8th & Str	C
5-29^{11}	5-16	F	30.57	76	4	4	3	3	1^1	30.57	7.10	Drove to win	D
5-24^1	5-16	F	30.36	75½	3	1	4	5	5^4	30.98	6.80	Trouble late	D
5-20^1	5-16	F	30.71	76	1	1	2	2	4^2	30.81	1.60	Contended to finish	D
5-15^{11}	5-16	F	30.86	75	3	4	2	3	1^1	30.86	4.40	Slow start, came on	M

Figure 3.15–Greyhound's First Race at a Higher Grade

In this example, Max's Dingo won a C grade race and then ran its first race in B company. The crowd bet it down to almost even money, regardless of the fact that it had never run at B grade before. It was obviously not ready for the higher class dogs and ran 6th.

Similar to maiden winners, never play dogs in their first race at a higher grade because they may be outclassed.

Dogs Dropping in Grade

Dogs that drop in grade are obviously out of form and therefore look bad on paper. For this reason the crowd usually allows them to go off at greater odds than they actually should. Considering that this same crowd over-plays recent winners going up in grade, **class droppers** make the very best bets.

Let's look at the effective class of a **grade riser** and a dropper. Today's race is at B grade. Midnight Kid is an effective C grade animal that will be running B grade for the first time.

5

MIDNIGHT KID												68	(10)	Kennel: AAA Racing, Inc. Trainer: S.C. Hanson Owner: M. Jones	
$4\text{-}23^{11}$	5-16	F	31.61	67	2	2	1	2	1^4	32.15	3.50	Dictated pace-rail			C
$4\text{-}19^{2}$	5-16	F	31.42	$67^{1/2}$	2	2	2^1	3	3^2	31.42	6.70	Held show			C
$4\text{-}15^{11}$	5-16	F	31.83	$67^{1/2}$	1	1	4	5	5^3	32.29	2.20	Bumped at 1/8th			C
$4\text{-}11^{5}$	5-16	F	31.53	68	1	1	2	2	2^4	32.04	7.60	Followed pace ins			C
$4\text{-}\ 8^{7}$	5-16	F	31.94	68	8	8^1	7	5	4^1	32.10	9.80	Steady improvement			C
$4\text{-}\ 3^{13}$	5-16	F	31.61	67	6	6	4	4	4^5	32.31	8.40	Never prominent			C
$3\text{-}30^{10}$	5-16	F	31.35	67	3	3	4	4	6^5	32.48	6.30	Forced wd at finish			C
$3\text{-}26^{9}$	5-16	F	31.47	68	2	2	4	6	8^9	32.76	1.50	Fell at 1/8th			C
$3\text{-}21^{11}$	5-16	F	31.73	$67^{1/2}$	4	4	3	3	1^1	31.73	7.10	Dashed for win			D
$3\text{-}17^{13}$	5-16	F	31.52	$67^{1/2}$	1	1^1	4	5	5^4	31.92	6.80	Trouble late			D
$3\text{-}14^{12}$	5-16	F	31.56	68	1	1^2	2	2	4^2	31.85	1.60	Squeezed at rail			D
$3\text{-}\ 9^{7}$	5-16	F	31.19	67	4	4	2	3	1^1	31.19	4.40	Steady gain to win			M

Figure 3.16–Greyhound Rising in Class

On the next page, notice that Canine Candice is out of form and dropping in class.

6

CANINE CANDICE										68	(10)		Kennel: AAA Racing, Inc. Trainer: S.C. Hanson Owner: M. Jones
4-23^{11}	5-16	F	31.61	67	2	2	1	2	2^4	32.15	3.50	Followed pace-rail	C
4-19^2	5-16	F	31.42	67½	2	2^1	3	4^2		31.42	6.70	Lost show by head	B
4-15^{11}	5-16	F	31.83	67½	1	1	4	5	6^3	32.29	2.20	Bumped at 1/8th	B
4-11^5	5-16	F	31.53	68	1	1	2	2	5^4	32.04	7.60	Dropped off pace ins	B
4- 8^7	5-16	F	31.94	68	8	8^1	7	5	4^1	32.10	9.80	Steady improvement	B
4- 3^{13}	5-16	F	31.61	67	6	6	6	5	2^5	32.31	2.20	Drove inside to show	B
3-30^{10}	5-16	F	31.35	67	3	3	4	4	6^5	32.48	6.30	Forced wd at finish	B
3-26^9	5-16	F	31.47	68	2	2	5	6	1^9	32.76	1.50	Despite trouble	B
3-21^{11}	5-16	F	31.73	67½	4	4	3	3	4^1	31.73	7.10	Slowed at finish	B
3-17^{13}	5-16	F	31.52	67½	1	2^1	2	3	5^4	31.92	6.80	Trouble late	B
3-14^{12}	5-16	F	31.56	68	1	1^2	2	2	4^2	31.85	1.60	Squeezed at rail	A
3- 9^7	5-16	F	31.19	67	4	1	1	1	4^1	31.19	4.40	Too fast, tired	A

B

Figure 3.17 - Greyhound Dropping in Class

All other things being equal, Canine Candice should easily beat Midnight Kid. Based on effective class, Midnight Kid is a C grade, whereas Canine Candice is a B grade. This represents one full grade point difference, and is substantial. Midnight Kid also has never competed with B grade animals and his performance is untested.

DOGS FROM OTHER TRACKS

Now that you understand how to calculate the effective grade at your track, you must learn how to correctly identify the grade of animals shipping in from other tracks. You will then be able to adjust their grades in relation to your local dogs.

When a dog ships in from a different track, there are two things that must be considered: the quality or rating of the previous track, and how its grading system is organized. These two factors often give shippers at the new track an advantage or disadvantage that astute handicappers consider crucial information. Let's first look at how to rate the quality of other tracks and then deal with their grading systems.

Rating Other Tracks
The size and quality of a track dictates the class of its animals, because at larger tracks there is a larger betting crowd and consequently higher purses. Higher purses attract quality kennels which in turn breed dogs

that are stronger and faster.

It is important to note that when dogs race against each other day after day at the same track, the grade or quality of that track always remains the same, so an effective grade analysis works fine. It is only when a dog ships to a different track that it is necessary to evaluate whether it will have an initial advantage or disadvantage over the animals at the new track.

It is also necessary to understand that this advantage or disadvantage is normally short lived, because after their first race at the new track, the dog's abilities are now obvious to all of the betting public. It is therefore necessary to learn how to rate other tracks so you can be ready to take advantage of the crowds initial ignorance regarding shippers.

Below is a basic rating system that can be used to evaluate whether an animal is shipping from a stronger or weaker track. A rating of 1 (one) signifies the best tracks, while a rating of 5 (five) represents the smallest tracks. These ratings are found on most racing programs.

TRACK RATING CHART

Apache, AZ—5	Multnomah, OR—2
Bayard, FL—3	Naples-FM, FL—3
Belmont, NH—5	Orange Park, FL—3
Biscayne, FL—1	Palm Beach, FL—2
Black Hills, SD—5	Pensacola, FL—4
Bluffs Run, IA—3	Phoenix, AZ—3
Caliente, MX—5	Plainfield, CT—3
Cloverleaf, CO—2	Pueblo, CO—4
Daytona, FL—3	Raynham, MA—1
Dubuque, IA—3	Rock Mt., CO—3
Ebro, FL—4	St. Petersburg, FL—1
Flagler, FL—1	Sanford-OR, FL—3
Greenetrack, AL—4	Sarasota, FL—3
Green Mt., VT—5	Seabrook, NH—4
Hinsdale, NH—5	Seminole, FL—3
Hollywood, FL—1	Sodrac, SD—4
Interstate, CO—3	Southland, AR—1
Jacksonville, FL—3	Tampa, FL—1
Jefferson, FL—4	Tri-State, WV—3
Juarez, MX—5	Victoryland, AL—3
Laredo Downs, MX—5	Waterloo, IA—4
Lincoln, RI—1	Wheeling Downs, WV—3
Mile High, CO—1	Wonderland, MA—1
Mobile, AL—3	Yuma, AZ—5

In conjunction with this, let's now look at the second piece of information needed to calculate whether a shipper is truly going up or down in class. This information is the grading system used at the dog's previous track. The list of tracks and assigned grades on the following page clearly show how grades are defined. For example, another track's A grade may be the same as your AA grade, but it is still the top grade and should be used in the evaluation as such.

TRACK AND ASSIGNED GRADE CHART

TRACK	LOCATION	Abb.	GRADES
Corpus Christi	Texas	CC	AA A B C J D M
Apache	Arizona	AP	A B C D E M
Belmont	New Hampshire	BE	A B C D E M
Biscayne	Miami, FL	BI	A B C D E M
Black Hills	South Dakota	BH	A B C D E M
Bluffs Run	Cncl Blff, IA	BR	A B C D M
Cloverleaf	Loveland, CO	CL	A BB B C D M
Coeur d'Alene	Idaho	CD	A B C D M
Dairyland	Kenosha, WI	DP	A B C D E M
Daytona Beach	Florida	DB	A B C D E M
Dubuque	Iowa	DQ	A B C D E M
Ebro	Florida	EB	A B C D E M
Flagler	Miami, FL	FL	A B C D E M
Fox Valley	Kaukauna, WI	FV	A B C D E M
Geneva Lakes	Delevan, WI	GL	A B C D E M
Greenetrack	Eutaw, AL	GT	A B C D E M
Green Mountain	Pownal, VT	GM	AA B C D E M
Hinsdale	New Hampshire	HI	A B C D E M
Hollywood	Florida	HO	A B C D E M
Interstate	Byers, CO	IS	A BB B C D M
Jacksonville	Florida	JA	A B C D E M
Jefferson Co.	Monticello, FL	JC	A B C D E M
Key West	Florida	KW	A B C D E M
Lincoln	Rhode Island	LI	AA A BB B C M
Mile High	Commerce City, CO	MH	A BB B C D M
Mobile	Alabama	MO	A B C D E M
Multnomah	Fairview, OR	MU	A B C DD D M
Naples-Ft. Myers	Florida	NF	A B C D E M
Orange Park	Jacksonville, FL	OP	A B C D E M
Palm Beach	Florida	PB	A B C D M
Pensacola	Florida	PE	A B C D E M
Phoenix	Arizona	PH	A B C D M
Plainfield	Connecticut	PL	A B C D E M
Pueblo	Colorado	PU	A BB B C D M
Raynham-Taunton	Mass.	RA	A B C J D M
Rocky Mountain	Colo. Springs, CO	RM	A BB B C D M
St. John's	Bayard, FL	SJ	A B C D E M
St. Petersburg	Florida	SP	A B C D E M
Sanford-Orlando	Longwood, FL	SO	A B C D E M
Sarasota	Florida	SA	A B C D E M
Seabrook	New Hampshire	SE	A B C J D M
Seminole	Casselberry, FL	SM	A B C D E M
Sodrac	N. Souix City, SD	SC	A BB B C D M
Southland	W. Memphis, AR	SL	A B C D E M
Tampa	Florida	TP	A B C D E M
Tri-State	Cross Lane, WV	TS	AA A B C D M
Tucson	Arizona	TU	A B C D M
Victoryland	Shorter, AL	VL	A B C D E M
Waterloo	Iowa	WL	A BB B C D M
Wheeling Downs	Wheeling, WV	WD	AA A B C D M
Wichita	Kansas	WT	A B C D E M
Wisconsin Dells	Wisconsin	WI	A B C D E M
Wonderland	Revere, MA	WO	AA A B C J M
Woodlands	Kansas City, KS	WS	A B C D M
Yuma	Arizona	YU	A B C D E M

As you can see by looking at the chart, the order of grades vary significantly from track to track, thus making it impossible to know whether a shipper is changing class until the grade relative to the new track is determined.

You now have all of the information necessary to modify the effective grade of a shipper, so let's first determine the relative grade.

Determining Relative Grade

Below is a B grade animal shipping into Phoenix from Waterloo.

6

CANINE CANDICE									68	(10)	Kennel: AAA Racing, Inc. Trainer: S.C. Hanson Owner: M. Jones

4-23^{11}	5-16	F	31.61	67	2	2	1	2	2^4	32.15	3.50	Followed pace-rail	B
4-19^2	5-16	F	31.42	67$^{1/2}$	2	2	2^1	3	4^2	31.42	6.70	Lost show by head	B
4-15^{11}	5-16	F	31.83	67$^{1/2}$	1	1	4	5	6^3	32.29	2.20	Bumped at 1/8th	B
4-11^5	5-16	F	31.53	68	1	1	2	2	3^4	32.04	7.60	Dropped off pace ins	B
4- 8^7	5-16	F	31.94	68	8	8	7	5	4^1	32.10	9.80	Steady improvement	B
4- 3^{13}	5-16	F	31.61	67	6	6	6	5	2^5	32.31	2.20	Drove inside to show	B

Figure 4.1–B Grade Dog Shipping fromWaterloo Racetrack

Uninformed players would assume that the Waterloo dog was an effective B grade animal, based upon its past performances. In fact, relative to Tucson, it is really only C caliber and will probably demonstrate this in its first out against Tucson B grades.

Phoenix	A	B	**C**	D		M
Waterloo	A	BB	**B**	C	D	M

If the Waterloo dog had been previously running BB races, it would then be comparable to a Phoenix B grade animal, but it wasn't.

Using another example, a Wheeling Downs A grade would only be a Phoenix B grade as you can see on the Track and Assigned Grade Chart. Wheeling Downs uses AA to represent their highest grade, rather than A.

MIRACLE FLEET   77   (8)   Kennel: AAA Racing, Inc.
                                                                      Trainer: S.C. Hanson
                                                                      Owner: M. Jones

3

Date		Track			Time								Fin			
8-31 [10]	WD	5-16	F	30.07	77	5	8	8	4	3^3	30.32	3.90	Wd 1st, late drv	A
8-27 [10]	WD	5-16	F	30.54	77	5	5	6	7	7^{11}	31.33	3.50	Wd 1st, trbl frtrn-in	A
8-22 [7]	WD	5-16	F	30.34	77	8	4	4	3	2^3	30.54	1.10	Dspt trouble frtn-in	A
8-17 [7]	WD	5-16	F	30.33	76	2	8	7	6	5^9	30.98	1.70	W 1st, bumped-md	A
8-11 [7]	WD	5-16	F	30.35	77	6	7	6	5	3^3	30.56	1.10	Overcm hit 1st-in	A
8- 7 [10]	WD	5-16	F	30.08	76	7	6	5	3	1^2	30.08	2.20	Wd 1st, str cmmnd	A

Figure 4.2–Grade A Dog Running at Wheeling Downs Racetrack

Phoenix	A	**B**	C	D	M
Wheeling	AA	**A**	BC	D	M

By using the grade chart you will be able to correctly identify what grade corresponds to your local grade for shippers and correctly convert the effective grade.

Using Ratings in Conjunction with Different Grades
After you have converted the grade, you must decide if it needs to be modified due to strength differences at the shipper's local track. On the track ratings chart, Waterloo has a ranking of four and Phoenix has a ranking of three, so BB grade dogs shipping into Phoenix have a mild class advantage over local B grade animals.

Wheeling Downs is rated as a three, the same as Phoenix, so you would only need to make sure that the grade difference was correct. (Remember, the Wheeling Downs A grade is the same as a Phoenix B grade).

Calculating the New Effective Grade

To make it easy let's use the same dog that shipped from Waterloo and is running its first race at Phoenix. We will first determine its comparable grade and then check the rating of both tracks.

6

CANINE CANDICE   68   (10)   Kennel: AAA Racing, Inc.
Trainer: S.C. Hanson
Owner: M. Jones

4-23[11]	5-16	F	31.61	67	2	2	1	2	2[4]	32.15	3.50	Followed pace-rail	B
4-19[2]	5-16	F	31.42	67 1/2	2	2	2[1]	3	4[2]	31.42	6.70	Lost show by head	B
4-15[11]	5-16	F	31.83	67 1/2	1	1	4	5	6[3]	32.29	2.20	Bumped at 1/8th	B
4-11[5]	5-16	F	31.53	68	1	1	2	2	3[4]	32.04	7.60	Dropped off pace ins	B
4- 8[7]	5-16	F	31.94	68	8	8[1]	7	5	4[1]	32.10	9.80	Steady improvement	B
4- 3[13]	5-16	F	31.61	67	6	6	6	5	2[5]	32.31	2.20	Drove inside to show	B
3-30[10]	5-16	F	31.35	67	3	3	4	4	6[5]	32.48	6.30	Forced wd at finish	B
3-26[9]	5-16	F	31.47	68	2	2	5	6	1[9]	32.76	1.50	Despite trouble	B
3-21[11]	5-16	F	31.73	67 1/2	4	4	3	3	4[1]	31.73	7.10	Slowed at finish	B
3-17[13]	5-16	F	31.52	67 1/2	1	2[1]	2	3	5[4]	31.92	6.80	Trouble late	B
3-14[12]	5-16	F	31.56	68	1	1[2]	2	2	4[2]	31.85	1.60	Squeezed at rail	A
3- 9[7]	5-16	F	31.19	67	4	1	1	1	4[1]	31.19	4.40	Too fast, tired	A

Figure 4.3–Shipper Greyhound

Canine Candice has been running B grade races at Waterloo and is entered into a B grade race at Phoenix. The first thing you need to do is to check Waterloo's grading system and see if this animal would also be considered a B grade at Phoenix.

Grading System					
Phoenix	A	B	**C**	D	M
Waterloo	A	AA	**B**	C	D	M

If you have already written a B next to the shippers name, you must now change it because the dog is a C grade animal based upon the grading system at Phoenix.

6

CANINE CANDICE														68	(10)	Kennel: AAA Racing, Inc. Trainer: S.C. Hanson Owner: M. Jones	
4-23^{11}	5-16	F	31.61	67	2	2	1	2	2^4	32.15	3.50	Followed pace-rail	B
4-19^2	5-16	F	31.42	67½	2	2	2^1	3	4^2	31.42	6.70	Lost show by head	B
4-15^{11}	5-16	F	31.83	67½	1	1	4	5	6^3	32.29	2.20	Bumped at 1/8th	B
4-11^5	5-16	F	31.53	68	1	1	2	2	5^4	32.04	7.60	Dropped off pace ins	B
4- 8^7	5-16	F	31.94	68	8	8^1	7	5	4^1	32.10	9.80	Steady improvement	B
4- 3^{13}	5-16	F	31.61	67	6	6	6	5	2^5	32.31	2.20	Drove inside to show	B
3-30^{10}	5-16	F	31.35	67	3	3	4	4	6^5	32.48	6.30	Forced wd at finish	B
3-26^9	5-16	F	31.47	68	2	2	5	6	1^9	32.76	1.50	Despite trouble	B
3-21^{11}	5-16	F	31.73	67½	4	4	3	3	4^1	31.73	7.10	Slowed at finish	B
3-17^{13}	5-16	F	31.52	67½	1	2^1	2	3	5^4	31.92	6.80	Trouble late	B
3-14^{12}	5-16	F	31.56	68	1	1^2	2	2	4^2	31.85	1.60	Squeezed at rail	A
3- 9^7	5-16	F	31.19	67	4	1	1	1	4^1	31.19	4.40	Too fast, tired	A

C

Figure 4.4–Adjusting for Grade at Another Track

Determining Rating Change

The next step is to determine if there is a class change between the two tracks. Find Phoenix and Waterloo in the Track Rating Chart on page 24.

> **Track Ratings**
> Phoenix, AZ—3
> Waterloo, IA—4

Waterloo is rated 1 point higher than Phoenix.

Each point difference translates to one grade increment. Adding an increment to C makes it a C+, adding an increment to a C+ makes it a B-, and so on. Refer to the Effective Grade Chart on page 18 to understand the value of an increment.

```
┌─────────────────────────────────┐
│        Grade Increments         │
│         A            C-         │
│         A-           D+         │
│         B+           D          │
│         B            D-         │
│         B-           E+         │
│         C+           E          │
│         C            E-         │
└─────────────────────────────────┘
```

Since Waterloo is rated one point higher than Phoenix the shipper has a converted effective grade of C. The next grade above C on the Grade Increment Chart is C+, so that is the grade you will use to evaluate the dog in this race.

The effective grade of Canine Candice has now been adjusted to C+, based on the grade difference and track ratings.

CANINE CANDICE   **68**   **(10)**   Kennel: AAA Racing, Inc.
                                                          Trainer: S.C. Hanson
                                                          Owner: M. Jones

4-23^{11}	5-16	F	31.61	67	2	2	1	2	2^4	32.15	3.50	Followed pace-rail	B	
4-19^2	5-16	F	31.42	67$^{1/2}$ 2	2	2^1	3	4^2	31.42	6.70	Lost show by head	B	
4-15^{11}	5-16	F	31.83	67$^{1/2}$ 1	1	4	5	6^3	32.29	2.20	Bumped at 1/8th	B	
4-11^5	5-16	F	31.53	68	1	1	2	2	3^4	32.04	7.60	Dropped off pace ins	B	
4- 8^7	5-16	F	31.94	68	8	8^1	7	5	4^1	32.10	9.80	Steady improvement	B	
4- 3^{13}	5-16	F	31.61	67	6	6	6	5	2^5	32.31	2.20	Drove inside to show	B	
3-30^{10}	5-16	F	31.35	67	3	3	4	4	6^5	32.48	6.30	Forced wd at finish	B	
3-26^9	5-16	F	31.47	68	2	2	5	6	1^9	32.76	1.50	Despite trouble	B	
3-21^{11}	5-16	F	31.73	67$^{1/2}$ 4	4	3	3	4^1	31.73	7.10	Slowed at finish	B	
3-17^{13}	5-16	F	31.52	67$^{1/2}$ 1	2^1	2	3	5^4	31.92	6.80	Trouble late	B	
3-14^{12}	5-16	F	31.56	68	1	1^2	2	2	4^2	31.85	1.60	Squeezed at rail	A	
3- 9^7	5-16	F	31.19	67	4	1	1	1	4^1	31.19	4.40	Too fast, tired	A	

6

C+

Figure 4.5–Adjusting Grade for Track Rating

Race Information on Shippers

It is very difficult to get more than the last six races on shippers, so determining their effective grade will not be as accurate as it would be with more information. Regardless of this, follow the rules outlined in this chapter and you will have a substantial advantage over the rest of the crowd.

RECENT FORM

After determining the effective grade of local dogs and shippers, the next step is to find out how they have been running recently. All athletes, whether human or otherwise, exhibit peaks and valleys in their physical performance. How well a dog has run in its most recent race or races is often an indicator of how it will do next out. This is referred to as its **recent form**.

Figure 5.1–Cyclical Greyhound Performances

Lower Grade Animals

Some dogs, usually lower grade animals, never really go in or out of form. These animals occasionally win, but only if the race conditions are favorable to their running style and they are not interfered with by other dogs. Figure 5.2 is an example of what their form might look like.

6

DASHING DAN										75	(7-2)	Kennel: AAA Racing, Inc. Trainer: S.C. Hanson Owner: M. Jones

2-11^6	5-16	F	32.08	75	2	3	5	5	6^{14}	33.92	4.50	Blocked at each turn	D
2- 5^{7X}	5-16	F	31.87	75	4	6	6	5	3^2	32.37	5.20	Jammed 1st turn-in	D
1-27^{6S}	5-16	F	31.68	76	7	5	5	5	6$^{8\,1\,2}$	33.41	3.50	Bumped twice	D
1-25^7	5-16	F	31.36	75	3	6	6	7	5^7	33.60	2.20	No threat	D
1-18^6	5-16	F	31.72	75	1	4	2	1$^{1\,2}$	1^1	31.72	2.60	Took lead stretch	E
1-13^6	5-16	F	32.43	75	6	3	3	7	8^{10}	34.06	1.00	Much trouble stretch	E

Figure 5.2–Lower Grade Greyhounds and Recent Form

As you can see by the inconsistant finishes, recent form has nothing to do with Dashing Dan's performance in future races. Lower grade dogs must be judged by such factors as favorable box, running style or other types of analysis outlined in this book.

Higher Grade Animals

Recent form in higher grade animals provides valuable insight and should be used in your handicapping techniques. The example below shows a quality dog that appears to be coming back into good form.

2

MTN BELLE										64	(10)	Kennel: AAA Racing, Inc. Trainer: S.C. Hanson Owner: M. Jones

7- 4^8	5-16	F	30.66	64	2	3	2	2	2^1	30.75	6.40	Held strong place	A
6-30^1	5-16	F	30.59	65	8	6	4	3	3^3	31.36	8.60	Gaining late str-in	A
6-24^{1X}	5-16	F	31.43	64	7	5	5	5	6^6	32.12	7.40	No mishaps	A
6-19^{11}	5-16	F	31.04	63	3	6	6	7	5^4	31.86	9.40	Hit 1st, up str-in	A
6-14^8	5-16	F	30.29	64	1	4	2	1$^{1\,2}$	2$^{1\,1\,2}$	30.58	6.10	Bumped up 1st-md	A
6-10^2	5-16	F	30.59	64	6	3	3	2	1$^{1\,2}$	30.59	12.60	Drove up strongly-in	B

Figure 5.3–Greyhound Coming Back Into Form

Notice that six races back the dog won a B grade race, came in second at A grade and then drifted out of form. After running the next two races 5th and 6th, the dog again appears to be coming back into form, finishing second last out. If this animal follows it's typical pattern it should be in good form for the next race.

Animals Dropping in Grade

The most profitable use of recent form is to find a dog that has dropped in class, run poorly, and then suddenly showed signs of life.

5

JAKE'S GOLD									**75**	**(5-2)**	Kennel: AAA Racing, Inc. Trainer: S.C. Hanson Owner: M. Jones	

8-31^{9x}	5-16	F	30.31	75	2	3	2	2	2^1	30.51	6.20	Held advantage-in	C
8-25^{7x}	5-16	F	30.60	76	8	6	5	6	4^5	31.48	7.00	Ran wide from start	C
8-21^{9x}	5-16	F	30.49	76	7	5	5	5	6^8	31.52	4.20	Never prominent	C
8-16^1	5-16	F	30.29	74	3	6	6	7	5^6	31.30	5.60	Wd 1st, never rcvd	B
8-11^1	5-16	F	30.24	75	1	4	2	4	4^3	31.24	8.80	Hampered early-md	B
8- 7^{9x}	5-16	F	30.72	74	6	3	3	5	8^9	31.88	6.00	trffc, bumped str	B

Figure 5.4–Grade Dropper Coming Alive

It appears that with another solid effort against C grade animals Jake's Gold has the class to win. If we could analyze races that he ran prior to the one's on the recent program, we would have even more insight into the dog's potential.

Analyzing Grade and Form

As was mentioned in earlier chapters, it is very productive to look at races that the dog has run prior to the last six races that appear on the program. This will give you a much better idea of whether an animal coming into form can compete against today's grade. Figure 5.5 shows the last twelve races of Prancin' Pluto.

7

PRANCIN' PLUTO   78   (6)   Kennel: AAA Racing, Inc. / Trainer: S.C. Hanson / Owner: M. Jones

Date	Dist		Time	Wt					Fin	Time	Odds	Comment	Gr
$9\text{-}30^7$	5-16	F	32.45	79	2	3	2	2	2^1	32.78	3.70	Held strong place-in	C
$9\text{-}26^8$	5-16	F	32.33	78	8	6	5	6	4^5	33.44	4.10	Crowded bk 1st-in	C
$9\text{-}21^{10}$	5-16	F	32.51	78	7	5	5	5	3^2	32.91	2.70	No mishaps on-rl	C
$9\text{-}17^{10}$	5-16	F	32.57	78	3	6	6	7	$5^{4\,1\,2}$	33.39	11.40	Cowded bk 2nd-in	B
$9\text{-}12^{10}$	5-16	F	32.99	$78^{1\,2}$	1	4	2	4	4^3	33.53	14.30	Followed leaders-in	B
$9\text{-}8^7$	5-16	F	32.43	79	6	3	3	5	8^9	33.46	2.00	Trffc 1st, bmpd-md	B
$9\text{-}3^{10}$	5-16	F	31.94	79	2	2	1^1	1^1	1^1	31.94	4.60	Extended for win	C
$8\text{-}29^{11}$	5-16	F	32.29	78	6	5	4	4	5^6	33.75	7.90	Wd 1st turn	B
$8\text{-}25^{14}$	5-16	F	32.58	77	8	8	7	7	6^7	33.82	4.50	Crowded 1st turn	B
$8\text{-}21^8$	5-16	F	32.22	78	1	3	3	3	4^3	33.14	1.30	Little change	B
$8\text{-}16^{10x}$	5-16	F	32.99	$78^{1\,2}$	5	3	$1^{1\,2}$	1^1	1^2	32.99	2.40	Caught midtrack 1st	C
$8\text{-}12^{10}$	5-16	F	32.38	77	2	2	3	3	2^1	32.76	6.80	Good drive at finish	C

Figure 5.5–Greyhound Exhibiting Strength in C Grade

By looking at races further back in time the running pattern of this dog becomes apparent. It is unable to beat B grade dogs but is an effective C grade contender. This dog is coming into form and should be competitive in today's C grade race.

Recent Form and Trouble

The final piece of information necessary to make sense out of recent form is whether the dog ran into trouble while coming into form.

8

SATIN BREEZE   61   (4)   Kennel: AAA Racing, Inc. / Trainer: S.C. Hanson / Owner: M. Jones

Date	Dist		Time	Wt					Fin	Time	Odds	Comment	Gr
$2\text{-}4^2$	5-16	F	32.98	$61^{1\,2}$	2	3	2	8	8^6	34.12	4.60	Knocked down str	A
$1\text{-}29^3$	5-16	F	32.26	61	6	4	3	3^2	32.96	5.30	Good effort ins	A
$1\text{-}22^3$	5-16	F	33.24	61	7	5	5	5	6^4	34.35	3.70	Never prominent	A
$1\text{-}16^2$	5-16	F	33.20	61	3	6	6	7	$5^{3\,1\,2}$	34.21	1.80	Wd 1st turn	A
$1\text{-}13^1$	5-16	F	32.39	$60^{1\,2}$	1	4	2	1	1^1	32.39	2.40	Up in stretch ins	A
$1\text{-}9^5$	5-16	F	31.96	$61^{1\,2}$	6	3	3	2	2^1	32.27	6.50	Steady effort midtrk	B

Figure 5.6–Greyhound Exhibiting Trouble Coming into Good Form

In this example, Satin Breeze appeared to be coming back into form and then ran 8th in the last race. The fact that the dog has class and was coming back into form before being "knocked down in the stretch" last out, indicates it might still be in good enough form to win the next race.

Recent Form Analysis

There is no need to calculate form on animals that are severely outclassed. Determining the recent form on dogs that have an effective grade three or more increments lower than today's grade is a waste of time. These dogs are not contenders in the race and should be eliminated from contention.

The dog below probably will not have enough class to compete with today's B grade animals that it has never faced before.

BETTY'S SONG										77	(6)	Kennel: AAA Racing, Inc. Trainer: S.C. Hanson Owner: M. Jones	
9-29⁶	5-16	F	32.96	77	7		4	4	1¹	32.96	5.50	Won in final stride	C
9-25⁹	5-16	F	32.83	76	4	7	5	4	2²	32.92	6.00	Steady effort inside	C
9-18¹²ˣ	5-16	F	32.59	77	6	5	4	3	2²	32.75	10.00	Closed gap inside	C
9-12¹	5-16	F	32.35	77	2	7	5	5	5⁸	32.91	6.30	Evenly after break	C
9- 5⁹	5-16	F	32.96	76	5	5	3	4	5¹⁰	33.67	9.70	Jammed 1st turn	C
8-30¹ˣ	5-16	F	32.63	77	2	4	2	2	1¹	32.63	3.50	Stretch win inside	D

Figure 5.7–Non-Competitive Dog Crossed Out

Evaluating Recent Form

The easiest way to evaluate **recent form** is to look at the finish position, grade and comment section of the last three races. Races prior to that are not necessary because they do not represent recent form.

Positive Recent Form

Below is an example of a dog that is coming into form.

DURANGO										**68**	**(3)**	Kennel: AAA Racing, Inc. Trainer: S.C. Hanson Owner: M. Jones	
7-26^{12}	5-16	F	40.48	69	3	2	1	2	2^1	40.73	8.70	Good early foot	C
7-20^{12}	5-16	F	40.45	68	5	7	6	5	4^3	40.96	9.50	Bumped 1st turn	C
7-15^{12}	5-16	F	40.48	67 ^{12}6	6	5	6	7^9		41.42	11.20	No factor	C

Figure 5.8–Greyhound Exhibiting Positive Recent Form

Durango finished 7th, then 4th, and in its last race, 2nd.
It is getting stronger and should be a factor.

Neutral Recent Form

The form on this dog cannot be accurately determined.

JILL'S JACKPOT										**81**	**(9-2)**	Kennel: AAA Racing, Inc. Trainer: S.C. Hanson Owner: M. Jones	
9-26^9	5-16	F	32.83	80	2	5	7	7	6^7	33.85	7.60	No threat	C
9-20^{9x}	5-16	F	32.66	80	3	4	4	4	3^4	33.17	9.30	Bumped early	C
9-15^1	5-16	F	32.69	81	5	6	5	4	5^6	33.54	6.80	No excuses	C

Figure 5.9 —Greyhound Exhibiting Neutral Recent Form

Jill's Jackpot is neither in or out of form based on her last
three races.

Poor Recent Form

Gatorman will soon be running one grade lower.

GATORMAN										**55**	**(11)**	Kennel: AAA Racing, Inc. Trainer: S.C. Hanson Owner: M. Jones	
10-2^1	5-16	F	32.76	54	4	1	3	6	7^8	34.15	13.20	No trouble	C
9-26^9	5-16	F	32.83	54	7	8	4	6	5^5	33.89	9.50	Jammed 1st turn	C
9-20^{7x}	5-16	F	32.69	55	1	2	2	2	2^1	32.94	7.90	Nosed out	C

Figure 5.10–Greyhound Exhibiting Poor Recent Form

The dog was in form three races ago but appears to be out now.

An analysis of the three dogs illustrates that Durango is probably in good enough form to be very competitive in today's C grade race, Jill's Jackpot is a question mark, and Gatorman is out of form and probably not a factor.

Remember, it is important that you analyze the grade along with the form, because higher class dogs can still be competitive at a lower grade even if they're not in their best form. This is especially true if they got into trouble their first race at the lower grade like the example below.

4

| PEPPERED | | | | | | | | | | | | | 60 | (7-2) | Kennel: AAA Racing, Inc. Trainer: S.C. Hanson Owner: M. Jones |

9-11^5	5-16	F	32.76	61	2	8	7	7	7^9	34.26	3.10	Bumped, never recvd	C
8-30^4	5-16	F	32.59	60	8	3	2	3	3^2	32.78	7.50	Good finish midtrack	B
8-25^5	5-16	F	32.63	60	5	4	5	5	4^3	32.97	8.40	Followed pace	B

Figure 5.11–Grade Dropper Interfered with First Out

Marking Your Program
There are four marks used to designate a dog's recent form. Let's use the four dogs we analyzed in this chapter to make it easy.

2

| DURANGO | | | | | | | | | | | | | 68 | (3) | Kennel: AAA Racing, Inc. Trainer: S.C. Hanson Owner: M. Jones |

7-26^{12}	5-16	F	40.48	69	3	2	1	2	2^1	40.73	8.70	Good early foot	C
7-20^{12}	5-16	F	40.45	68	5	7	6	5	4^3	40.96	9.50	Bumped 1st turn	C
7-15^{12}	5-16	F	40.48	67	6	6	5	6	7^9	41.42	11.20	No factor	C

Figure 5.12–Marking a Greyhound in Good Recent Form.

5 | **JILL'S JACKPOT** | **81** | **(9-2)** | Kennel: AAA Racing, Inc.
Trainer: S.C. Hanson
Owner: M. Jones

$9\text{-}26^9$	5-16	F	32.83	80	2	5	7	7	6^7	33.85	7.60	No threat	C
$9\text{-}20^{9x}$	5-16	F	32.66	80	3	4	4	4	3^4	33.17	9.30	Bumped early	C
$9\text{-}15^1$	5-16	F	32.69	81	5	6	5	4	5^6	33.54	6.80	No excuses	C

Figure 5.13–Marking a Greyhound Whose Form is Undetermined.

8 | **GATORMAN** | **55** | **(11)** | Kennel: AAA Racing, Inc.
Trainer: S.C. Hanson
Owner: M. Jones

$10\text{-}2^1$	5-16	F	32.76	54	4	1	3	6	7^8	34.15	13.20	No trouble	C
$9\text{-}26^9$	5-16	F	32.83	54	7	8	4	6	5^5	33.89	9.50	Jammed 1st turn	C
$9\text{-}20^{7x}$	5-16	F	32.69	55	1	2	2	2	2^1	32.94	7.90	Nosed out	C

Figure 5.14 - Marking a Greyhound Who is Out of Form

4 | **PEPPERED** | **60** | **(7-2)** | Kennel: AAA Racing, Inc.
Trainer: S.C. Hanson
Owner: M. Jones

$9\text{-}11^5$	5-16	F	32.76	61	2	8	7	7	7^9	34.26	3.10	Bumped, never recvd	C
$8\text{-}30^4$	5-16	F	32.59	60	8	3	2	3	3^2	32.78	7.50	Good finish midtrack	B
$8\text{-}25^5$	5-16	F	32.63	60	5	4	5	5	4^3	32.97	8.40	Followed pace	B

Figure 5.15–Marking a Grade-Dropping Greyhound With Interference

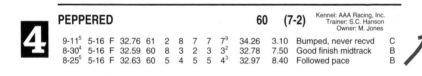

Recent Form will be used to separate contenders
later in the analysis section.

SPEED

The next step is to find out which dogs have been running the fastest times at today's distance. Although speed is only one factor in racing, dogs that have the ability to reach the finish line ahead of the field have a distinct advantage.

Speed ratings are accomplished by comparing dogs' final times against the track records. The most productive strategy is to analyze the three most representative races. This gives you an **Average Speed** score which shows you the animals that have a speed advantage.

Analyzing Speed
There are three pieces of information that you must look at in order to calculate a dog's Average Speed score. They are the **distance, grade** and **actual time**. The distance and grade of previous races are only used to determine which final times are included in the analysis.

6

DASHING DAN 75 (7-2) Kennel: AAA Racing, Inc.
Trainer: S.C. Hanson
Owner: M. Jones

2-11^6	5-16	F	32.08	75	2	3	5	5	6^{14}	33.92	4.50	Blocked at each turn	D
2- 5^{7X}	5-16	F	31.87	75	4	6	6	5	3^2	32.37	5.20	Jammed 1st turn-in	D
1-27^{5S}	5-16	F	31.68	76	7	5	5	5	6$^{8\,1\,2}$	33.41	3.50	Bumped twice	D
1-25^7	5-16	F	31.36	75	3	6	6	7	5^7	33.60	2.20	No threat	D
1-18^6	5-16	F	31.72	75	1	4	2	1$^{1\,2}$1^1	31.72	2.60	Took lead stretch	E	
1-13^6	5-16	F	32.43	75	6	3	3	7	8^{10}	34.06	1.00	Much trouble stretch	E

Figure 6.1–Location of Distance, Actual Times, and Grades

Using Today's Distance

In order to understand a dog's speed potential for today's race, previous races at exactly today's distance must be used in your calculations. If a dog ran a different distance than today's distance in one of its last three races, disregard that race and use the next older race at today's distance.

5

WORLD CLASS 72 (7-2) Kennel: AAA Racing, Inc.
Trainer: S.C. Hanson
Owner: M. Jones

2- 6^6	5-16	F	31.17	72	3	8	7	7	6^8	32.24	6.60	Ran wide, trouble	B
2- 1^{7X}	5-16	F	31.46	71	6	3	4	5	5^7	32.89	9.70	Good early effort	B
1-28^{5S}	3-16	F	18.82	72	7	4	6	7	8^9	19.98	3.40	No contender	B
1-23^7	5-16	F	31.99	72	5	5	3	2	1^1	31.99	6.10	Strong finish, inside	C
1-19^6	5-16	F	31.75	72	1	2	2	2$^{1\,2}$3^2	32.04	3.10	Edged out of Place	C	
1-16^6	5-16	F	31.48	70	6	5	2	2	2$^{1\,1\,2}$	31.57	6.90	Steady effort, mdtrk	C

Figure 6.2–Exclude Races of Different Distances

In the example above, World Class ran at 3/16 of a mile three races ago. This race should not be used to determine its speed, assuming it is running 5/16 of a mile today. Use the 5/16 race below which is equal to today's distance.

Grade Considerations

The following are examples of how grade, in conjunction with distance, determines which races should be used for consideration in evaluating Average Speed scores. There will always be situations that do not fit any of these examples and will require common sense. When in doubt, use the last three races at today's distance.

Dogs Running in a Competitive Grade

The dog below is an effective C grade animal running a 5/16 race at C grade. This is what 90% of your races will look like. Simply use the last three races to determine the Average Speed.

7

WIZARD OF PAWS									**75**	**(10)**	Kennel: AAA Racing, Inc. Trainer: S.C. Hanson Owner: M. Jones		
4-25^9	5-16	F	31.17	75	8	6	7	7	8^8	33.01	7.30	Slight bump 1st turn	C
4-22^3	5-16	F	31.46	76	6	5	4	3	3^2	32.89	6.10	Strong effort to show	C
4-18^{13}	3-16	F	18.82	76	6	4	4	3	2^1	33.07	6.60	Steady gain, inside	C
4-13^{13}	5-16	F	31.99	75^{12}	2	2	2	3	3^1	32.99	5.90	Held on to show	C
4- 8^1	5-16	F	31.75	75	5	6	5	5^{12}	4^2	33.04	8.40	Trouble , never recv'd	C
4- 3^1	5-16	F	31.48	74	4	4	3	3	4^{112}	32.58	9.00	Lost show, tired late	B

Figure 6.3 - Determining Average Speed from the Last 3 Races

An exception would be if the animal was interfered with and ran a second or more slower than normal in one of its last three races. If this was the case, use the next most recent race at today's distance.

4

TIGER TAIL									**62**	**(10)**	Kennel: AAA Racing, Inc. Trainer: S.C. Hanson Owner: M. Jones		
2- 6^2	5-16	F	32.05	62	7	5	8	7	8^{17}	33.99	9.40	Bumped, trouble	B
1-31^2	5-16	F	32.16	62	4	6	7	7	7^{11}	32.77	8.20	No contender	B
1-27^4	5-16	F	32.09	61^{12}	5	2	2	3	4^5	32.49	10.30	Spd to stretch, Mdtrk	B
1-22^{11}	5-16	F	32.85	61^{12}	6	2	2	2	1^1	32.85	7.60	Ups in stretch, ins	C
1-15^{13}	5-16	F	32.75	61	4	2	4	4^{12}	3^5	33.38	6.90	Even effort, mdtrk	C
1- 9^1	5-16	F	32.53	61	5	4	2	3	3^{612}	32.95	11.40	Good effort, mdtrk	C

Figure 6.4—Greyhound that was Interfered with in Last Race

Tiger Tail was bumped in its last race and finished over a second slower than the previous three races. That race is therefore thrown out of your calculations.

Dogs That Failed in Higher Grades

Many dogs run inconsistently when they are outclassed. After winning a race, dogs must run the next three or four races with better animals. Often they are intimidated and fail to compete.

Below is an example of a dog that won a C grade race and has been unsuccessfully running with B grade animals the last three outs.

BAJA BRAT   **80   (8-2)**   Kennel: AAA Racing, Inc.
Trainer: S.C. Hanson
Owner: M. Jones

10-8⁵	5-16	F	30.86	76	7	6	4	5	6⁷	32.24	6.60	Pushed outside	B
10-5²	5-16	F	31.12	76	3	7	4	5	5⁵	32.89	8.30	Knocked down 1st trn	B
10-2⁹	5-16	F	31.27	76	5	6	7	7	8⁹	33.07	7.50	Traffic, slowed up	B
9-30¹²	5-16	F	31.99	76	2	1	1	1	1¹	31.99	3.40	Box to wire	C
9-27⁴	5-16	F	31.75	75	3	1	2	2¹²	3²¹²	32.04	4.10	Edged for show, str	C
9-23¹¹	5-16	F	31.40	74¹²	4	4	3	2	2¹	31.57	6.70	Settled for place	C

Figure 6.5—Greyhound Unsuccessful at a Higher Grade

After Baja Brat won the C grade race he was forced to compete with higher classed B grade animals. Note that against B grade animals his fastest time was 32.24. This is slower than any of his previous C grade times.

If today's race is with B grades, use the last three B grade races in order to calculate the average speed. This is due to the fact that the dog will probably perform the same today as he did in his previous races against the higher grade animals.

BAJA BRAT												80	(8-2)	Kennel: AAA Racing, Inc. Trainer: S.C. Hanson Owner: M. Jones	
$10\text{-}8^5$	5-16	F	30.86	76	7	6	4	5	6^7	32.24	6.60	Pushed outside			B
$10\text{-}5^2$	5-16	F	31.12	76	3	7	4	5	5^5	32.89	8.30	Knocked down 1st trn			B
$10\text{-}2^9$	5-16	F	31.27	76	5	6	7	7	8^9	33.07	7.50	Traffic, slowed up			B
$9\text{-}30^{12}$	5-16	F	31.99	76	2	1	1	1	1^1	31.99	3.40	Box to wire			C
$9\text{-}27^4$	5-16	F	31.75	75	3	1	2	2^{12}	3^{212}	32.04	4.10	Edged for show, str			C
$9\text{-}23^{11}$	5-16	F	31.40	74^{12}	4	4	3	2	2^1	31.57	6.70	Settled for place			C

Figure 6.6—Calculate Average Speed Using Today's Grade (B)

If today's race is C grade (instead of a B), use only the final times posted at C grade, even though those races were run a while back. The dog will probably at least match his previous C grade times when facing animals that he has already beaten.

BAJA BRAT												80	(8-2)	Kennel: AAA Racing, Inc. Trainer: S.C. Hanson Owner: M. Jones	
$10\text{-}8^5$	5-16	F	30.86	76	7	6	4	5	6^7	32.24	6.60	Pushed outside			B
$10\text{-}5^2$	5-16	F	31.12	76	3	7	4	5	5^5	32.89	8.30	Knocked down 1st trn			B
$10\text{-}2^9$	5-16	F	31.27	76	5	6	7	7	8^9	33.07	7.50	Traffic, slowed up			B
$9\text{-}30^{12}$	5-16	F	31.99	76	2	1	1	1	1^1	31.99	3.40	Box to wire			C
$9\text{-}27^4$	5-16	F	31.75	75	3	1	2	2^{12}	3^{212}	32.04	4.10	Edged for show, str			C
$9\text{-}23^{11}$	5-16	F	31.40	74^{12}	4	4	3	2	2^1	31.57	6.70	Settled for place			C

Figure 6.7–Calculate Average Speed Using Today's Grade (C)

Remember to always disregard speed scores achieved by animals that *failed* at a grade higher. This is because they do not represent the dog's potential at their effective grade.

Competitive Dogs in Higher Grade

If a dog has at least one 3rd place finish or better at the higher grade, it is acceptable to use the three most recent races, regardless of grade.

TICK TOCK 71 (2) Kennel: AAA Racing, Inc.
Trainer: S.C. Hanson
Owner: M. Jones

4

5-14^2	5-16	F	30.86	71	4	2	2	2	2^1	31.44	5.90	Followed pace, ins	B
5- 9^8	5-16	F	31.12	71	2	4	3	3	3^2	31.69	4.60	Bumped mdtrk 1st trn	B
5- 6^{11}	5-16	F	31.27	70	^{12}7	5	3	2	1^{12}	32.07	6.50	Drove to win, ins	C
5- 1^3	5-16	F	31.99	71	3	6	6	3	2^2	31.99	7.30	Carried wd, good fin	C
4-26^3	5-16	F	31.75	70	1	7	3	3^{12}	4^5	32.04	6.80	Despite trouble	C
4-22^7	5-16	F	31.40	71	2	4	4	4	3^4	31.57	9.10	Pushed back 1st turn	C

Figure 6.8–Calculate Average Speed with 3rd Place Finish or Better

Tick Tock is obviously competitive at higher grades based on his last two finishes. In this example use the last three races to evaluate his speed.

Calculating Average Speed

After you have determined which races are satisfactory to use in your calculations, draw a line under them. The dog below is easy because it is running a B grade race today and all of its past races are at 5/16.

RD'S MAGIC 61 (5-2) Kennel: AAA Racing, Inc.
Trainer: S.C. Hanson
Owner: M. Jones

2

7-19^{13}	5-16	F	31.19	60	3	1^2	6	5	4^5	32.21	8.60	Trouble mdtrack	B
7-15^{13}	5-16	F	31.25	61	6	3	5	4	5^6	32.29	2.20	Pinched back late	B
7-12^2	5-16	F	30.88	61	3	1	2	2	2^1	31.07	6.40	Followed pace, ins	B
7- 8^2	5-16	F	31.96	61	1	5	4	4	4^3	32.49	3.00	Bumped 1st turn	B
7- 5^{11}	5-16	F	31.74	61	1	2	2	2	3^2	32.04	2.50	Edged out of place	B
7- 2^{14}	5-16	F	31.57	60	^{12}2	2	1^1	1^1	1^{112}	31.57	4.70	Took control after 1st	C

Figure 6.9–Calculating Average Speed

After you have underlined the last three finish times, add them up and divide by three to get the average speed.

Add Last 3 Races	32.21
	32.29
	+ 31.07
	95.57
Divide by 3	95.97 divided by 3 = **31.86**

The next step is to subtract the average from the track record in order to get the difference. The track record is the fastest time recorded at that distance.

Average Speed	31.86
Track Record	- 30.56
Difference	1.30

The final calculation is to multiply the difference times 10 in order to make it a whole number.

Multiply	1.30
Difference	x 10
By 10	13.0

The dog's average speed is thirteen and this should be written next to the final times column. It will be used later in the analysis.

RD'S MAGIC |3 **61** **(5-2)** Kennel: AAA Racing, Inc. / Trainer: S.C. Hanson / Owner: M. Jones

7-19^{13}	5-16	F	31.19	60	3	1^2	6	5	4^5	32.21	8.60	Trouble mdtrack	B
7-15^{13}	5-16	F	31.25	61	6	3	5	4	5^6	32.29	2.20	Pinched back late	B
7-12^2	5-16	F	30.88	61	3	1	2	2	2^1	31.07	6.40	Followed pace, ins	B
7- 8^2	5-16	F	31.96	61	1	5	4	4	4^3	32.49	3.00	Bumped 1st turn	B
7- 5^{11}	5-16	F	31.74	61	1	2	2	2	3^2	32.04	2.50	Edged out of place	B
7- 2^{14}	5-16	F	31.57	60	^{12}2	2	1^1	1^1	1^{112}	31.57	4.70	Took control after 1st	C

Figure 6.10–Marking Average Speed on Your Racing Program

A score of zero is the best score possible. A dog would have to equal the track record in each of its last three races to achieve that score.

When you analyze a race, you will use these numbers to rank the speed of each dog. Higher grade dogs will have lower numbers (because they ran closer to the track record) and lower grade dogs will have higher numbers, but how a dog's score relates to the other dogs in its race is the most important thing.

RUNNING STYLE

The configuration of the track, the box and how these factors relate to each dogs' running style greatly influences the outcome of a race. By studying these variables you will be able to successfully predict how each animal should react to the racing conditions.

Where Calls Are Made

The first thing that you must understand is how to identify **call positions**. They are different for each track and also for each course at each track. The call positions are important because they determine how a dog's running style will be affected by the layout of each course.

Except for distances of 3/16 or less you will always have a **Start**, **1/8th**, **Stretch** and **Finish** call. Learn how to quickly find them on your program and also where the calls are made at each course.

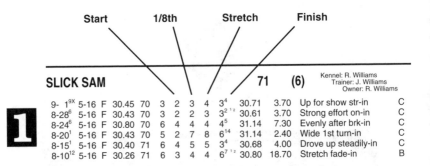

Figure 7.1–Location of Calls

At Southland Greyhound Track, for example, the **break call** is made just as the greyhounds leave the starting box. The **second call** is made one eighth (1/8) of a mile later and is at different points on the track depending on which course is run. The **stretch call** is made at the same point for all distances, just as they enter the final turn (except Crittenden Course, see example). The finish line and corresponding **final call** is also the same for each course.

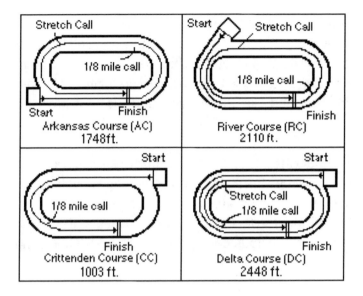

Figure 7.2–Location of Track Calls

As you can see, the starting position of a race varies according to which course is being run. In very short races the start is critical because if there is early bumping, the dog that should have won the race may not have time to recover.

Learn each course at your track and study how the dogs typically negotiate the start and turns. Make a note of which courses demand early speed and which ones reward a strong close. There will be a course that will allow a front runner to easily grab the lead or a closer the distance necessary to pass the rest of the tiring front runners. You will benefit from this knowledge.

Win Percentage by Box

Dogs learn a running style at an early age and typically maintain it until they quit racing. A dog's starting position is known as a **box**. About one third prefer inside boxes, another third like the outside and the rest have no preference.

The main thing to understand is that regardless of which box produces the highest win percentage at your track, dogs must still be evaluated based on which box fits their running style. Figure 7.3 is an example of wins per box from the four courses at Southland Greyhound Track.

1	246	4	20	270
2	200	2	26	228
3	183	1	15	199
4	199	3	12	214
5	148	1	8	157
6	141	2	13	156
7	135	0	8	143
8	165	1	13	179

Figure 7.3–Course Win Per Box at Four Course

The chart illustrates the **Wins Per Box** out of each box

on all four courses. The inside boxes, along with the very outside box produced the highest win percentages. The box the dog starts from, its individual running style, and the length of the race all affect these percentages.

Typically, the shorter the course, the more dramatic the box bias, because dogs have less time to recover from being bumped or to get inside or outside. A dog breaking from an unfavorable box in a race 3/16 of a mile or less is normally at a real disadvantage.

6

LA FEVER   **73**   **(3-1)**   Kennel: R. Williams / Trainer: J. Williams / Owner: R. Williams

1-16^6	3-16	F	19.25	72	8	7	6	8	8^9	21.24	4.40	Bumped wd 1st turn	AA
1-12^2	3-16	F	19.83	72	1·2 3	2	2	1^2	1^1	19.83	5.00	Steady drive outs	A
1- 9^9	3-16	F	19.67	73	8	8	4	5	5^7	20.34	6.30	Wide run	A
1- 5^{10}	3-16	F	18.31	73	6	6	8	7	6^8	19.98	4.70	Forced wide 1st	AA
1- 2^{10}	3-16	F	19.50	73	1^1	1^2	1^1	1^1	3^2	19.91	11.00	Outfinished mdtk	AA

Figure 7.4–Unfavorable Outside Box Position in a Shorter Race

---

A favorable box will occasionally allow a marginal animal the final edge necessary to win a race, but will usually not cause the best animal to lose. When you play lower grades, box bias becomes even more of a factor and can have a greater effect on the outcome because these dogs often do not have the strength or experience to compensate for an incompatible box.

Determining Front and Back Runners

Dogs not only develop tendencies to run inside and outside, but also prefer running in the front or back of the pack. In order to effectively evaluate each dogs' running style, you must first determine whether the animal is a front or back runner. The easiest way to do this is to look at the last six start calls.

Front Runner Start Call	Back Runner Start Call
3 1 4 2 3 6	6 4 8 7 5 8

Front runners consistently compete for the lead while back runners are content to run from behind. Neither running style is superior to the other but each is evaluated differently. Let's begin by analyzing the factors that effect front runners.

Inside/Outside Front Runners

The most important factor relating to front runners is whether they prefer to run on the inside or outside. In many programs, a chart is provided that has the basic running style of each dog. This will allow you to make a quick determination of whether the dog is an inside or outside runner. Using this information you will be able to simulate the race and hopefully discover if detrimental bumping might occur.

For handicappers that do not have this information, track position preference can be determined by looking at three sets of data on the dogs' charts: **box position**,

finish and **race comments**. These are found on your racing program as illustrated in Figure 7.5.

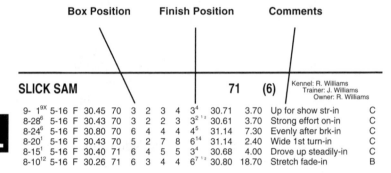

Figure 7.5–Locating Track Position Preference

The easiest way to determine if a dog is an inside or outside runner is to simply evaluate the race Comments, the Box Position and the Finish.

INSIDE RUNNING STYLE INDICATORS		
Box	**Finish**	**Comment**
1	1	Won easily
8	6	Trouble in lane
7	7	Bumped, wide
3	2	No trouble
7	8	Bumped 1st turn
2	1	Evenly inside

As you can see, the dog in the above example consistently performed better from the inside. When starting from the inside, no problems were encountered; when starting from the outside, the dog bumped other dogs trying to get inside.

OUTSIDE RUNNING STYLE INDICATORS

Box	Finish	Comment
7	1	Won easily
2	6	Trouble in lane
1	7	Bumped, wide
8	2	No trouble
3	8	Bumped 1st turn
6	1	Evenly inside

This dog above is an obvious outside runner.

NO PREFERENCE RUNNING STYLE INDICATORS

Box	Finish	Comment
1	1	Won easily
8	6	Trouble in lane
7	7	Bumped, wide
8	2	No trouble
7	8	Bumped 1st turn
7	1	Evenly inside

Box position does not affect this animal so it is considered to have no preference. These dogs are classified as "Neither".

Race Evaluation Using Running Style
After you have defined the running styles of each dog, evaluate the running style of the entire race using all of the dogs.

Evaluation of an entire race with no running style problems:

Box	Comment
1	Neither
2	Inside
3	Neither
4	Neither
5	Neither
6	Neither
7	Outside
8	Neither

In this example, regardless of which dog or dogs you are playing, running style should have little bearing on the outcome of the race.

Evaluation of a race with running style problems:

Box	Comment
1	Neither
2	Inside
3	Neither
4	Neither
5	Neither
6	Neither
7	Neither
8	Inside

In the second example, dog #8 will probably try to get inside after the start, which could cause a significant amount of bumping. If dogs #5, #6, or even #7 are contenders and like to run on the front, make sure they show enough early speed to break ahead and out of the way of a possible bump by dog #8.

Each race can have many variations of running style problems. It makes it easier to visualize if you create a chart similar to the one below.

This illustration shows how a dog running from box number 1 and a dog running from box number 8 would normally run their race if they both had an inside running style. As you can see, dog number 1 would probably have very little trouble, whereas dog number 8 would probably bump several dogs trying to get inside.

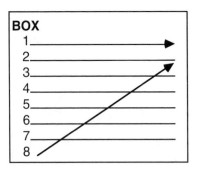

Figure 7.6 - Running Style Chart

Determining Early Speed Rating
In the context of running style, good **early speed** often neutralizes the negative influence of a poor or non-compatible box for front runners. Therefore, after you have determined each dog's box preference, it is a good idea to calculate the early speed rating.

Using the 1st call from the program, look at how well each dog normally starts the race. If a dog consistently exhibits good early speed he can often escape both bumping and being bumped. The start position of each of the last six races will provide you with this information.

Start

SLICK SAM															71	(6)	Kennel: R. Williams Trainer: J. Williams Owner: R. Williams	

9- 1^{9X}	5-16	F	30.45	70	3	2	3	4	3^4	30.71	3.70	Up for show str-in	C
8-28^6	5-16	F	30.43	70	3	2	2	3	3$^{2\,1\,2}$	30.61	3.70	Strong effort on-in	C
8-24^6	5-16	F	30.80	70	6	4	4	4	4^5	31.14	7.30	Evenly after brk-in	C
8-20^1	5-16	F	30.43	70	5	2	7	8	6^{14}	31.14	2.40	Wide 1st turn-in	C
8-15^1	5-16	F	30.40	71	6	4	5	5	3^4	30.68	4.00	Drove up steadily-in	C
8-10^{12}	5-16	F	30.26	71	6	3	4	4	6$^{7\,1\,2}$	30.80	18.70	Stretch fade-in	B

Figure 7.7–Starting Position of Last 6 Races

After examining the last six races for each dog, decide which animals exhibit "identifiable" early speed. Do this by averaging the last six starts. If the dog averages 3 or less in its first call over the last six races, it can be considered to have superior early speed.

CALCULATING EARLY SPEED RATING

1
3
2
1
2
1

These Starts represent a dog that exhibits **Superior** early speed.

1	These Starts represent a
8	dog that exhibits **Average**
4	early speed.
2	
6	
5	

8	These Starts represent a
7	dog that exhibits **Poor**
8	early speed.
6	
4	
7	

Step I
Add last six Start calls.

$$
\begin{array}{r}
2 \\
2 \\
4 \\
2 \\
4 \\
+\ 3 \\
\hline
17
\end{array}
$$

Step II
Divide by 6   17 divided by 6 = **2.8**

This dog shows excellent early speed. Animals that exhibit poor early speed are very possibly middle or back runners and require a different analysis. This is explained later.

Early Speed Strategy
Several race simulations will now be illustrated. Using a combination of box, running style and early speed you will be able to determine whether bumping will likely occur, and to which animals.

EXAMPLE OF RACE WITH NO LIKELY BUMPING

BOX	COMMENT	EARLY SPEED	RATING
1	Neither	Average	(4)
2	Neither	Average	(3.8)
3	Neither	Average	(4.5)
4	Neither	Average	(3.9)
5	Neither	Average	(5)
6	Neither	Average	(4)
7	Neither	Average	(4.2)
8	Inside	Superior	(1.6)

In this example, dog #8 will probably not bump this group while trying to get inside based upon his superior early speed. If dog #8 was the dog that you liked to win this race, his early speed would serve to neutralize the detrimental inside running style.

To make it even simpler, round off early speed averages. If a score is less than .5, round down. If it is .5 or over, round up. For example: 3.5 = 4, and 3.4 = 3.

**EXAMPLE OF A RACE WITH
OUTSIDE TO INSIDE BUMPING**

Box	Comment	Early Speed
1	Neither	3
2	Inside	6
3	Neither	4
4	Neither	2
5	Neither	5
6	Neither	6
7	Neither	2
8	Inside	4

In this race, dog #7 could still prove to be a contender, but dogs #5 and #6 are likely to get bumped and should be evaluated in such terms. (Note that rounded figures are being used for the early speed rating.)

**EXAMPLE OF A RACE WITH
INSIDE TO OUTSIDE BUMPING**

Box	Comment	Early Speeed
1	Outside	7
2	Inside	4
3	Neither	6
4	Neither	6
5	Neither	2
6	Neither	5
7	Neither	7
8	Neither	2

In this similar situation, dog #1 could cause severe bumping on his way outside.

Box	Comment	Early Speed
EXAMPLE OF CROSS BUMPING		
1	Outside	3
2	Inside	6
3	Neither	4
4	Neither	2
5	Neither	5
6	Neither	6
7	Neither	2
8	Inside	4

The first dog that dog #1 will probably bump should be dog #3 because dog #2 does not have very strong early speed and likely will be behind dog #1 when he begins to turn outside. Dog #4 should be just fine and probably will be running in the lead with dog #7.

To successfully handicap a race it is necessary to determine the running style of each animal in each race. This is crucial to anticipating any trouble that might affect the dogs you are wagering on. If running problems may affect your contenders, do not play that race.

Marking Your Form
After you have determined the running style of each dog it is necessary to mark your program so the information is readily available when you prepare to do your final race analysis. Every animal must be evaluated regard-

ing running style because even non-contenders have an effect on other dogs in the race.

Determining Qualifying Dogs

If a dog has a score of four or lower in the Early Speed Analysis then it can be assumed that it will at least try for the lead when it breaks. A score of four is between Superior and Average as represented in the Early Speed Analysis example charts.

1
3
2
1
2
1

These Starts represent a dog that exhibits **Superior** early speed.

1
8
4
2
6
5

These Starts represent a dog that exhibits **Average** early speed.

Next to each animal in the program mark their running style (Inside/Outside/Neither) and Early Speed Average.

First decide their style:

Inside = I
Outside = O
Neither= N

Then add the Early Speed Average: I - 2

Place this information above the start column as shown in Figure 7.8, so it can be used in the evaluation.

5

GYPSY MOON	**F I-2**								60	(10)	Kennel: R. Williams Trainer: J. Williams Owner: R. Williams
3- 1^9	5-16	F	39.53	55	1	1	3	2	3^1	39.62	25.10	Challenged hard str	C
2-26^6	5-16	F	39.11	56^{12} 8	2	3	5	8^{14}	40.10	8.60	Wide early, faded-in	C
2-22^6	5-16	F	39.26	56	3	3	2	1	1^{12}	40.08	13.00	Bumped esc turn-md	C
2-19^9	5-16	F	39.27	56	1	1	5	6	$6^{7\,z}$	39.75	25.70	Never improved-in	B
2-15^8	5-16	F	30.28	56^{12} 7	1	7	7	7^{12}	31.14	11.60	Wd 1st, bumped-in	B
2-11^4	5-16	F	30.46	57	6	4	5	5	5^8	31.03	14.10	Evenly after break	B

Figure 7.8–Marking Running Style and Early Speed Average

Gypsy Moon is a front (F) inside (I) runner with an early speed rating of two.

Middle and Back Runners

In the previous examples, each dog's running style has been analyzed in relation to early speed and front-end bumping. Before you finish with running style you must also look at dogs that are not interested in competing for, or running on the lead.

These **middle and back runners** do not contest the lead, but instead run from behind. They do not normally get into early trouble (like the inside and outside runners mentioned earlier), but can still experience difficulty because they must eventually pass half or more of the field in order to win the race.

These **back runners**, dogs that run from behind, are evaluated using two factors, how fast they reach the 1/8th call and how well they finish. Dogs that reach the 1/8th pole consistently on top, and then run strong to the finish, must always be considered a strong contender even though they do not contest the early lead. Figure 7.9 represents what a solid back runners' last six races might look like.

CJ'S DREAM														**62**	**3**	Kennel: R. Williams Trainer: J. Williams Owner: R. Williams
4-24^5	5-16	F	31.57	62	6	6	1^1	1$^{2\,2}$1^4	31.57	5.60	Won easily	C
4-19^2	5-16	F	32.26	61$^{1\,2}$	8	8	2	3	3^2	32.49	9.20	Trouble in lane	C
4-15^5	5-16	F	31.49	61	6	5	3	3	7^5	36.71	4.10	Bumped, wide	C
4-10^1	5-16	F	31.84	62	3	2	3	2	2$^{1\,2}$	31.96	10.30	No trouble	C
4- 5^{3s}	5-16	F	32.35	61$^{1\,2}$7	8	4	3	8^7	37.52	3.70	Bumped 1st turn	C
3-15^4	5-16	F	31.60	62	5	6	2	3	3^4	32.64	6.70	Evenly inside	C

Figure 7.9–Dog Exhibiting a "Back" Running Style

As you can see, this dog does not contend for the early lead, but its closing ability still makes it a very good bet.

An interesting fact is that middle and back runners consistently have higher payouts than front runners, even if they both have a similar winning record. The crowd seems to love front runners and always bets them accordingly. Professional handicappers keep a keen eye for consistent back runners and capitalize on the higher odds.

Determining Back Runners

Back runners race differently than front runners and therefore must be analyzed using other criteria. Unlike front runners, there is no need to worry about whether they prefer to run on the inside or outside. Their position at the 1/8th pole and their closing ability determine how they are evaluated.

Analyze their 1/8th speed score and finish score using the same format that you used to find the early speed score for front runners. The only difference is that you will not round off the scores. The reason is that closing ability deals in fractions, which are substantially affected if reduced or expanded during rounding.

Below is an example of a back runner that is a good closer. By looking at its start calls, you can see that it is obviously not a front runner.

LONE STAR LASS   **56**   **(5-2)**   Kennel: R. Williams / Trainer: J. Williams / Owner: R. Williams

7

7-	2^9	5-16	F	39.97	55	6	6	3	3	2^1	40.12	8.40	Late drv to chllng-rl	B
6-24^{8x}		5-16	F	39.89	55	7	8	4	4	4^6	40.83	3.60	Moved up, tired-ins	B
6-12^9		5-16	F	39.82	55	6	5	2	2	1^1	39.82	4.00	Off last, drew off-rl	C
6-	5^9	5-16	M	39.21	55	8	7	4	3	2^2	39.95	5.20	Came on strong str	C
5-31^9		5-16	F	39.36	56	7	6	3	3	3^4	40.47	4.90	Split trffic frtn-ins	C
5-28^9		5-16	F	39.27	55	5	5	2	2	$2^{1\,1\,2}$	39.56	8.00	Drove up gamely-rl	C

Figure 7.10–Greyhound Exhibiting a Back Runner Style

Analyzing Back Runners

Below are three steps that are necessary to determine how well a back runner peforms.

Step I

The first step is to average the 1/8 call times. If a dog has an average 1/8th call score of 3.0, this is considered very good (a score of 4 or lower is above average). To calculate this score you simply add all of the 1/8th calls (3+4+2+4+3+2=18) and divide by 6. (The computation is similar to what you did to determine Early Speed.)

Step II

The next step is to find the finish call average. Add up all of the finish calls (2+4+1+2+3+2=14) and divide by 6. This average is 2.3.

Step III

Finally, subtract the finish call average from the 1/8th call average to get the dog's closing ability.

$$
\begin{array}{r}
3.0 \\
-\ 2.3 \\
\hline
+\ .7
\end{array}
$$

This dog has a 3.0 average 1/8th call and a +.7 closing ability. These are excellent scores making the animal a very good back runner and contender if its class and other factors are acceptable. You will use these numbers in your final analysis.

Let's look at another dog that also has poor early speed but is not really an effective back runner because of its inability to close.

SAMBA BLAZE **60** **(8)** Kennel: R. Williams
Trainer: J. Williams
Owner: R. Williams

3

2-	6^{11}	5-16	F	31.39	61	7	6	4^1	5	5^6	32.65	11.70	No threat	C
2-	2^{11}	5-16	F	32.08	61^{12}	8	8	6	6	6^9	33.21	8.70	Followed pace	C
1-28^4		5-16	F	31.98	61	6	5	3	3	3^3	32.48	3.30	Steady gain mdtrk	C
1-24^7		5-16	F	31.74	61	7	7	4	4	5^7	33.06	6.90	Squeezed at finish	C
1-20^7		5-16	F	32.16	60^{12}	5	6	6	6	6^8	33.83	9.20	Forced wide 1st turn	C
1-16^6		5-16	F	31.81	59	5	5	6	7	7^{11}	34.07	7.50	Jammed midway	C

Figure 7.11–Back Runner that Fails to Close

By observing the dog's average start it is obvious that this animal does not run to the front. Let's now evaluate the average 1/8th and finish call to find out if it is a good back runner.

First, add all of the 1/8th calls and divide by the number of calls.

$$4+6+3+4+6+6 = 29$$
$$29 \text{ divided by } 6 = \textbf{4.8}$$

This gives you an average 1/8th call of 4.8, which is below average.

Now add the finish calls and divide by the number of finish calls.

$$5+6+3+5+6+7 = 32$$
$$32 \text{ divided by } 6 = \textbf{5.3}$$

The final procedure is to find the **closing ability** by subtracting the finish call from the 1/8th call.

$$\begin{array}{r} 4.8 \\ -\ 5.3 \\ \hline -\ .5 \end{array}$$

This dog's average 1/8th call is poor and he also a shows a negative closing ability. Lone Star Lass (the first dog analyzed) demonstrated much stronger closing ability, which is the most important factor with back runners.

Mark these figures next to each back runner so they can be used later in the analysis. Use the letter B to signify middle or back runners, and place the average 1/8th finish next to it. Then add the close. Below is a back runner (B) with an average 1/8th of 5 and a -.5 closing ability.

SAMBA BLAZE				**B5 -.5**				**60**		**(8)**	Kennel: R. Williams Trainer: J. Williams Owner: R. Williams

3

2- 6^{11}	5-16	F	31.39	61	7	6	4^1	5	5^6	32.65	11.70	No threat	C
2- 2^{11}	5-16	F	32.08	61^{12}	8	8	6	6	6^9	33.21	8.70	Followed pace	C
1-28^4	5-16	F	31.98	61	6	5	3	3	3^3	32.48	3.30	Steady gain mdtrk	C
1-24^7	5-16	F	31.74	61	7	7	4	4	5^7	33.06	6.90	Squeezed at finish	C
1-20^7	5-16	F	32.16	60^{18}	5	6	6	6	6^8	33.83	9.20	Forced wide 1st turn	C
1-16^6	5-16	F	31.81	59	5	5	6	7	7^{11}	34.07	7.50	Jammed midway	C

Figure 7.12 - Marking Running Style on Your Racing Program

KENNELS

Kennel Evaluation

You cannot use kennel evaluation as a primary handicapping system, but dogs from top kennels are worthy of consideration if they qualify as contenders using the other criterion outlined in this book. Examine your program and make a note of the top kennels at your track. These are the kennels that train and race the most winners and essentially have the best dogs. Figure 8.1 is an example of how kennel rankings appear in your program.

Kennel Standings Week Ending April 11, 1990					
Kennel#	Kennel	Starts	Wins	2nds	3rds
15	Duane Randle	696	117.5	108.5	101.0
20	Thunderbird Kennel, Inc.	607	96.0	73.5	90.0
8	Ron Dorsey	641	96.0	79.0	98.0
12	C. E. Mullen, Jr.	668	95.0	87.0	78.0
14	W. F. Muth, Inc.	663	93.0	89.0	71.0
9	Fickett Racing Kennel	665	84.5	86.5	74.0
11	Mrs. Robert Marriott	630	55.0	81.0	72.5
10	Darby K. Henry, Inc	625	70.0	83.5	104.5
19	Heatherbrook	556	78.5	71.5	76.5
6	Connell Kennels, Inc.	590	79.0	61.0	61.0
4	Mike Castellani, Inc.	576	73.0	87.0	80.5
17	John Seastrom	548	82.0	65.0	69.5
21	Max Trice	536	63.0	76.0	79.5
3	Carroll Blair	628	69.0	85.0	73.0
16	Ryan & Miller	524	56.0	56.0	73.5
1	E. J. Alderson	547	54.0	73.0	67.5
18	Shockley Kennels, Inc.	572	55.0	64.0	67.0
2	H. D. Beckner	457	52.0	59.0	48.0
24	Summit Farms	490	49.5	46.5	49.0
5	Deryl Clark	433	34.0	42.0	44.0
22	Arkansas Breeders	199	11.0	19.0	15.0

Figure 8.1 –List of Kennel Rankings

Kennels must be evaluated in regards to either **percentage of wins** or percentage of **in the money** (first, second and thirds). Using just the highest number of starts is not the best way to determine the top kennel because that number only suggests which kennel races the most dogs, not necessarily the best ones.

In order to find the percentage of wins, or percentage of "in the money," simply divide the number of starts into the wins or into a combination of firsts, seconds and thirds, depending on which percentage that you want.

For example, let's look at Duane Randle, the first kennel on our chart. This kennel has had 696 starts, posting 117.5 wins and a total of 327 races in the money.

Kennel#	Kennel	Starts	Wins	2nds	3rds
	Kennel Standings				
	Week Ending April 11, 1990				
15	Duane Randle	696	117.5	108.5	101.0
20	Thunderbird Kennel, Inc.	607	96.0	73.5	90.0
8	Ron Dorsey	641	96.0	79.0	98.0
12	C. E. Mullen, Jr.	668	95.0	87.0	78.0
14	W. F. Muth, Inc.	663	93.0	89.0	71.0

Figure 8.2–Top Ranked Kennel - Duane Randle

By dividing 696 into 117.5, you will find that dogs from this kennel won 17% of their races. Next, you can divide the total starts (696) into the number of times this kennel's dogs were in the money (327) to get a very respectable 47%.

Your betting style determines which percentage you are looking for. If you bet to win, kennels with the highest win percentages must be considered. If being in the money is more important because you specialize in trifecta or show tickets, kennels that get the most dogs in the money are more important.

Betting on a dog just because it comes from a good kennel is poor strategy. But, if a solid contender happens to also be from a highly ranked kennel, this dog is probably ready to race.

Rating Kennels

The best way to use kennel ratings in your analysis is to divide the kennels into five categories based on their win or in-the-money percentage.

Top 20%	**5**
2nd 20%	**4**
3rd 20%	**3**
4th 20%	**2**
Bottom 20%	**1**

Figure 8.3—Kennel Rating Chart

As you can see, top kennels receive a rating of five (5) with bottom kennels getting a one (1). Unlisted kennels at your track always receive a zero (0). Animals shipping in from other tracks should not receive any kennel score (including a zero) unless you have a kennel rating from that track.

Marking Your Program

Now mark each dogs' kennel rating next to the kennel on the program.

5

MARVIN'S CHAMP　　　　　　　　　　73　　(8)　　Kennel: Duane Randle　**K=5**
Trainer: S.C. Hanson
Owner: M. Jones

$10\text{-}2^8$	5-16	F	32.66	73	5	2	7	7	$7^{8\ 12}$	33.25	9.80	Crowded 1st turn	C
$9\text{-}26^{13}$	5-16	F	32.74	73	1	2	1	2	4^5	33.14	6.50	Forced early pace	C
$9\text{-}20^{6x}$	5-16	F	32.86	73	1	4	5	3	1^1	32.86	5.30	Won near wire inside	D
$9\text{-}12^1$	5-16	F	32.77	73	2	3	6	6	6^9	33.39	12.30	Crowded early	D
$9\text{-}\ 5^4$	5-16	F	32.70	74	3	8	7	6^{12}	6^{13}	33.65	5.50	Much early trouble	D
$8\text{-}29^5$	5-16	F	33.19	74	8	3	4	4	$3^{2\ 12}$	33.38	6.60	Forced wide bkstr	D

Figure 8.4 - Marking Kennel on Your Racing Program

Marvin's Champ is trained by a top kennel and therefore receives a rating of five. This Kennel Rating will be included in the dog's final score in the Analysis section of this book.

WINNING ANALYSIS

The factors that you have analyzed are **grade**, **recent form**, **speed**, **running style** and **kennel**. In order to handicap a race, it is necessary to translate these calculations into actual scores. These scores can then be used in the betting section.

Score Chart

The easiest way to compile the information into overall scores is to create a chart that contains all five categories. Below is an example:

Dog	Grade	Form	Speed	Run Style	Kennel	Tot Score	Adj Score
1							
2							
3							
4							

Figure 9.1 - Scoring Chart

Using this chart you will be able to quickly compile the scores for each animal in every race. The following four sample dogs will be used to help you understand the evaluation of each factor.

CANINE CANDICE B5 +.7 18 68 K=0 Kennel: Williams Co.
Trainer: S.Cibbs
Owner: W. Martin

1 ↓ B

5-11^{11}	5-16	F	30.96	67	1	5	4	4	6^8	32.31	6.30	Ran wide, never rcovrd	B
5- 8^2	5-16	F	31.04	67½	4	6	5	4	4^3	32.25	4.90	Never prominent	B
5- 4^{11}	5-16	F	31.12	67½	3	5	6	4	3^2	31.52	3.70	Steady gain to show	B
4-30^5	5-16	F	31.19	68	7	4	3	2	2^1	31.24	5.10	Couldn't catch winner	B
4-26^7	5-16	F	31.25	68	5	6	5	4	4^5	31.78	9.30	Tired at finish	B
4-22^{13}	5-16	F	31.37	67	8	7	7	6	7^9	32.47	8.50	Much trouble, 1st & Fin	B

SHOOTING ASTRO F I-2 15 62 K=3 Kennel: Johnson Dog Co.
Trainer: T. White
Owner: R. Barness

2 ↑ C+

5-11^1	5-16	F	30.76	61	5	2	2	2	3^4	31.33	6.70	Nosed out to show	B
5- 8^2	5-16	F	30.62	61	4	3	4	5	5^7	31.95	11.20	Ran wide	B
5- 4^{11}	5-16	F	31.40	61	6	1	1	1	1^2	31.40	4.80	Wide turns, breezed	C
4-30^{12}	5-16	F	30.94	60	3	3^1	3	5	4^5	31.78	3.50	Bumped down stretch	C
4-26^{8x}	5-16	F	30.89	60	6	2	2	3	3^2	31.28	3.00	Even effort	C
4-22^{12}	5-16	F	31.25	61	7	1	1	1	2^1	31.44	5.10	Came up short-ins	C

MIDNIGHT KID B4 -.3 21 68 K=1 Kennel: AAA Racing, Inc.
Trainer: S.C. Hanson
Owner: M. Jones

3 — C-

5-11^{11}	5-16	F	31.61	67	5	3	6	7	7^6	32.94	9.20	Never prominent	B
5- 8^2	5-16	F	31.42	67½	3	4	3^1	2	1^1	32.38	4.30	Steady gain	C
5- 4^{11}	5-16	F	31.83	67½	2	5	4	4	3^2	32.66	7.50	Followed pace	C
4-30^5	5-16	F	31.53	68	2	4	5	7	8^{10}	33.15	10.60	Slowed down at 1/8th	C
4-26^7	5-16	F	31.94	68	3	3	2	2	1^1	32.71	4.80	Stretch command-ins	D
4-22^{13}	5-16	F	31.61	67	4	3	4	5	6^4	32.83	6.40	Wide turns, stayed bk	D

BONA-FIDO F I-4 13 66 K=5 Kennel: AAA Racing, Inc.
Trainer: S.C. Hanson
Owner: M. Jones

4 ↑ B

5-11^{9x}	5-16	F	31.30	65	5	3	4	3	2^1	31.53	4.60	Mvd up after 1/8th	B
5- 8^2	5-16	F	31.38	65	2	4	3	3	3^4	31.69	6.10	Slow start, held on	B
5- 4^3	5-16	F	31.40	64½	3	2	2	6	4^5	32.36	5.20	Squeezed on rail, ins	B
4-30^3	5-16	F	31.56	65	5	8	6	4	2^1	31.84	9.50	Bumped, strong close	B
4-26^4	5-16	F	31.22	65	6	6^1	3	3	5^6	32.47	11.00	In trouble twice	B
4-22^3	5-16	F	31.75	66	2	3	3	2	1^1	31.75	8.70	Won driving	C

Figure 9.2 - Sample Greyhounds Used for Analysis

Analyzing Grades

You will always use the Effective Grade that was determined for each dog. If the dog was a **shipper**, (a greyhound whose previous race was run at a different track) the Relative Effective Grade is used.

Step One

Examine the Effective Grade of each dog on your program, this should be noted to the right of the grade column.

| BONA-FIDO | | | | | | | | | | 66 | (4-3) | | Kennel: AAA Racing, Inc. Trainer: S.C. Hanson Owner: M. Jones | |

6- 9^{9x}	5-16	F	31.30	65	3	3	4	3	3^2	31.86	6.60	Mvd up at 1/8th to Shw	C
6- 4^2	5-16	F	31.38	65	3	4	3	4	4^4	32.14	7.30	Late fade-ins	C
5-31^3	5-16	F	31.40	64½	6	2	2	3	6^7	32.73	7.20	Outrun at finish	B
5-26^3	5-16	F	31.24	65	8	1	4	5	2^2	31.59	8.70	Erratic outside	B
5-22^4	5-16	F	31.22	65	1	5^1	6	4	6^8	32.42	11.50	Ran wide, poor effort	B
5-17^3	5-16	F	31.18	66	2	8	7	7	7^9	32.93	3.40	Pinnd agnst rail 1st trn	B

Figure 9.3 - Dog with an Effective Grade of B

Bona-Fido has an Effective Grade of B. An Effective Grade must be calculated for each dog in the race.

Step Two

Using all of the dogs in the race, find the dog or dogs with the highest Effective Grade, and assign these dogs 50 points each. Dogs with lower Effective Grades are deducted 10 points per increment. (Use the Effective Grade Chart on page 30 to understand what an increment is.) Following is an example of how you would calculate points using the Grade Increment Chart for the sample dogs.

PARTIAL GRADE INCREMENT CHART

B	=	50	(Highest Grade)
B-	=	40	
C+	=	30	
C	=	20	
C-	=	10	

Notice that Canine Candice and Bona-Fido both have an Effective Grade of B, which is the top grade in this sample. They receive 50 points each. Ten points are then deducted for each increment lower, giving Shooting Astro a grade score of 40, and Midnight Kid a 10.

The highest Effective Grades in each race always receive 50 points, regardless of what the grade is. This is because the grades in each race are relative only to the dogs in that particular race, not to the top possible grade at the track.

You can now fill in the first space on your Score Chart.

Dog	Grade	Form	Speed	Run Style	Kennel	Tot Score	Adj Score
1	50						
2	40						
3	10						
4	50						

Analyzing Form

The next score that you must generate relates to form. If you refer back to Chapter 5, there are four designations that represent a dog's recent form.

⌐	+ 10 Points	Good recent form.
↖	+ 5 Points	Interfered with while coming into form.
▬	0 Points	Undetermined recent form.
⌐	-10 Points	Poor recent form.

Using the same four dogs, fill in the correct number of points in the second category on your Score Chart.

Dog	Grade	Form	Speed	Run Style	Kennel	Tot Score	Adj Score
1	50	-10					
2	40	+10					
3	10	0					
4	50	+10					

Analyzing Speed

Speed is calculated like grade in the sense that you will again be looking for the top dog or dogs. The dog with the LOWEST speed rating number has the best speed score because it ran the least amount of time off the track record. The lowest speed rating score receives 30 points, and the others are deducted 3 points per speed rating point higher. Below are the speed scores for our example dogs.

Dog	Speed Score	Speed Points
1	18	15
2	15	24
3	21	9
4	13	30

Dog #4 had a speed score of 13, which was the lowest and best of the group. He receives the most amount of points, which is 30.

Dog #2 had the second best score. It was two speed points slower than the best score so you multiply 2 x 3 = 6 and subtract that from 30, which equals 24.

Dog #1 had the third best score which was five speed points slower than the top score. Multiply 5 x 3 = 15, and subtract this number from 30. This gives you a score of 15 points.

Dog #3 posted the worst speed rating score of the group. It was seven points off the best score and therefore received 9 points for speed (7 x 3 = 21 subtracted from 30 equals 9).

You can now fill in the Score Chart.

Dog	Grade	Form	Speed	Run Style	Kennel	Tot Score	Adj Score
1	50	-10	15				
2	40	+10	24				
3	10	0	9				
4	50	+10	30				

Analyzing Running Style

In order to evaluate running style you must first look at your notations to see if the dog is a front or back runner. If the dog is a front runner (F) then today's box and the early speed rating are evaluated. Back runners (B) receive points based on their ability to get to the 1/8th pole and their closing ability. Neither style is any better than the other, therefore both types of runners can earn score points in the analysis.

Front Runners

The notation below signifies a front runner (F), the part of the track it prefers (I = Inside) and it's early speed rating (2).

FI - 2

Step One

The first step in determining a dog's score for running style is to look at the box it is breaking from in relation to its running style. In the following chart are the points that will be awarded or deducted based on its running style and box.

RUNNING STYLE CHART FOR FRONT RUNNERS

Box	Running Style (Inside)	Running Style (Outside)	Running Style (Neither)
1	10	-10	0
2	10	-10	0
3	5	-5	0
4	0	0	0
5	0	0	0
6	-5	+5	0
7	-10	+10	0
8	-10	+10	0

Notice that inside runners running from the inside receive positive points along with outside runners running from the outside. Dogs running from incompatible boxes are penalized points.

Step Two

The next step is to see if the dog's early speed is good enough to reduce any negative points it received due to a poor box. If a dog scored less than 4 on its early speed rating, or received a neutral or positive running style score, disregard this step.

Only animals with negative scores use early speed to adjust their negative running style points. This is because they can normally outrun early trouble and should not be penalized as seriously as front runners that show poor early speed and are running from a box that is incompatible.

EARLY SPEED ADJUSTMENT CHART

Early Speed Score	Running Style Points	Adjusted Points
1	-10	0
2	-10	0
3	-10	-5
4	-10	-10
1	-5	0
2	-5	0
3	-5	0
4	-5	-5

Match up the dog's Early Speed Score in the left hand column with the Running Style points in the middle column. This will give you the adjusted points in the right-hand column. Dog #2 and dog #4 in our example are both front runners so let's analyze their scores.

Dog #2 is an inside runner with an Early Speed Score of 2. Based on the Running Style Chart, it will get 10 points for starting from the inside (#2 box). There is no adjustment because it received positive points.

Dog #4 is an inside runner with an Early Speed Score of 4 and receives 0 points for running style because it is starting from the four box. This score would not be adjusted because it received neutral (0), not negative points.

Back Runners

Back runners are scored using a combination of their speed to the 1/8th and their close. Their 1/8th score indicates how fast they get to the 1/8th call in relation to the other back runners, while their closing ability is the difference between their last six 1/8th and finish calls.

An example of a back runner's notation would be B3 .7. This dog is a back runner (B), has a 1/8th call score of 3 and a closing ability of .7.

Step One

In the first part of the calculation, points are awarded to those animals that get to the 1/8th call the quickest. This involves simply subtracting the 1/8th call score from 10, like in the example below.

$$B\boxed{3}.7 \qquad \begin{array}{r} 10 \\ -\ 3 \\ \hline 7 \end{array}$$

The 1/8th call points in this example are 7, which will be combined with the close call points.

Step Two

The second calculation is to identify the dog or dogs with the best closing ability and award the close call points.

$$\text{B3}\boxed{.7}$$

This will either be the largest positive number or smallest negative number. The best closer (and any dogs that tie it) will receive a score of 20 points. The remaining animals will lose 1 point for every .1 points less than the top score.

To get a feel for the calcuation, let's look at an example of four backrunners' closing scores and their accompanying points. (These are different dogs than we are following in our sample.)

Dog	Closing Score	Points
5	.8	20
6	-.2	10
7	.5	17
8	-.7	5

Dog **#5** had the best closing score (.8), and therefore receives the highest number of points (20).

Dog **#7** was .3 points lower than the top and therefore receives 17 points (20 - 3).

Dog **#6** had a negative closing score of -.2, which was 10 full points lower then the top closing score, so he gets a score of 10 (20 - 10).

Dog **#8** had the worst closing score and receives a total of 5 points for this category (20 - 15).

By adding up the 1/8th Call score and close call points, you get the correct number of points toward back runners.

Calculating Running Style for Sample Dogs
Let's now calculate the running style points of our four sample dogs. Dog **# 1** is a back runner (B5 .5) and has the top closing score of .5. He will therefore receive 5 points for 1/8th call (10-5) and 20 points for having the best closing ability (.5).

Dog **#2** is an inside front runner (FI - 2) and receives 10 points for being an inside runner breaking from the #2 box. This is taken directly from the Running Style Chart listed earlier in this chapter.

Dog **#3** is a back runner (B4-.3) and receives 6 points for 1/8th call (10 - 4) and 12 close call points (20 - 8), because it is .8 lower in close than the top dog (dog #1).

Dog **#4** is a front runner (FI - 4) breaking from the #4 box, and therefore receives 0 running style points.

Let's now add the points to our Score Chart.

Dog	Grade	Form	Speed	Run Style	Kennel	Tot Score	Adj Score
1	50	-10	15	20			
2	40	+10	24	10			
3	10	0	9	18			
4	50	+10	30	0			

Analyzing Kennel

The final factor is kennel and it is a very easy calculation. Simply add the kennel rating that each dog received to the Score Chart.

CANINE CANDICE B5 $^+$.7 18 68 K=0   Kennel: Williams Co.
Trainer: S.Cibbs
Owner: W. Martin

5-11[11]	5-16	F	30.96	67	1	5	4	4	6[8]	32.31	6.30	Ran wide, never rcovrd	B
5- 8[2]	5-16	F	31.04	67½	4	6	5	4	4[3]	32.25	4.90	Never prominent	B
5- 4[11]	5-16	F	31.12	67½	3	5	6	4	3[2]	31.52	3.70	Steady gain to show	B
4-30[5]	5-16	F	31.19	68	7	4	3	2	2[1]	31.24	5.10	Couldn't catch winner	B
4-26[7]	5-16	F	31.25	68	5	6	5	4	4[5]	31.78	9.30	Tired at finish	B
4-22[13]	5-16	F	31.37	67	8	7	7	6	7[9]	32.47	8.50	Much trouble, 1st & Fin	B

Figure 9.4 - Noting Kennel Score for Canine Candice

Notice that Canine Candice has a kennel score of 0 (K = 0).

Dog	Grade	Form	Speed	Run Style	Kennel	Tot Score	Adj Score
1	50	-10	15	20	0		
2	40	+10	24	10	3		
3	10	0	9	18	1		
4	50	+10	30	0	5		

Total Scores

Now add up all of the scores in order to get the Total Score.

Dog	Grade	Form	Speed	Run Style	Kennel	Tot Score	Adj Score
1	50	-10	15	20	0	75	
2	40	+10	24	10	3	87	
3	10	0	9	18	1	38	
4	50	+10	30	0	5	95	

Adjust Highest Scores

Adjust the highest score so that it equals 100. Dog #4 has the highest score (95) so add 5 points.

Dog	Grade	Form	Speed	Run Style	Kennel	Tot Score	Adj Score
1	50	-10	15	20	0	75	
2	40	+10	24	10	3	87	
3	10	0	9	18	1	38	
4	50	+10	30	0	5	95	100

Adjust All Scores

Now, add the same amount of points that you added to the top dog (5), to all of the other scores. If the top dog has a score over 100, deduct the amount of points necessary to make it's score 100, and deduct the same amount from all other dogs. The top dog's score must always equal 100 in order to accommodate the betting analysis.

Dog	Grade	Form	Speed	Run Style	Kennel	Tot Score	Adj Score
1	50	-10	15	20	0	75	80
2	40	+10	24	10	3	87	92
3	10	0	9	18	1	38	43
4	50	+10	30	0	5	95	100

You are now ready to use these scores.

BETTING

Wagering at the Track

How you wager at the track is just as important as selecting the best dogs. This can be demonstrated with a story that you have probably heard a hundred times. A player corners you at the ticket window and brags about how he picked ten winners on yesterday's program. You ask him how much money he made, expecting to hear about his new car or boat. He then gets sheepish and admits that he actually broke even because he parlayed all of his winnings on a 5-1 shot in the last race. You guessed it, the dog ran fourth but should have won.

In this chapter you will learn the correct ways to wager your money and the most effective bets toward making you a winner.

The Tote Board

I consider the tote board to be more of a negative influence on greyhound handicappers than alcohol or even tout sheets. The board reflects the opinion of the betting public. The problem is they are incorrect two out of every three races!

The betting public are the same gamblers that have a "lucky" three number box and play it in every race, regardless of which dogs are wearing the numbers. They also tend to rely heavily on birthdays, colors and an assortment of other irrational nonsense. By allowing the tote board to influence your bets, you are accepting their silly methods.

For example, people who play the tote board favorite to win every race will lose about 17% of their money. By betting the first and second choices in the Quinella, they will still end up with a net loss of about 13%. This is a little better than the 20% normally lost by simply flipping a coin, but it still doesn't make very good sense.

Each race must be analyzed using the guidelines outlined in this book, and the key dogs and top contenders bet according to their scores. The only time the tote board should be an influence is if the odds on a dog drop so low that the reward does not justify the risk.

Track Take and Breakage
Tracks take an average of 17% to 20% out of each betting pool for straight bets, and even more for the exotics. This is called the **track take** or **take**. That means that 80% or less of the money is paid back to the bettors. Hypothetically, you should not lose more than 20% of what you bet, but we know that isn't always true.

When playing favorites, "breakage" is another factor that reduces the payoff. **Breakage** is the difference between the actual money in the pool and the final payout to the winners. It occurs because the total money bet, divided by the number of winning tickets, is usually not an even amount. For this reason, tracks round down to the nearest dime when they determine the final payoff.

What this means to you is, if a dog's actual payoff should have been $2.28 for a ticket, holders of the ticket will get $2.20 instead. With long odds winners, breakage isn't very meaningful, but ticket holders on favorites lose a large percentage of what their payoff should have been.

These are the built-in losses that every player must contend with when they go to the track. It takes solid handicapping and correct betting to overcome the money given up to track take and breakage.

Types of Bets

There are many different types of bets, but for simplicity, let's categorize them into straight and exotic. Win, Place and Show are the **straight bets** and all of the others are defined as **exotic**. The first thing you must learn is the best strategy for straight bets. Then you will be ready to play the most popular exotic, the Trifecta.

Standard Bets

The three straight wagers that you can bet are for the dog to **Win** (first), **Place** (second) or **Show** (third). If you play to *win*, the dog must finish first in order for you to cash the ticket. If the dog finishes first or second it qualifies as a *place*. A *show* wager allows the dog to finish in either of the top three positions.

All three bets are effective if they are used in the correct circumstances. The next section will define the best strategy for these types of bets.

Betting to Win

Professional handicappers will typically bet to win on the best dog in the race if it has a distinct advantage over the rest of the field. A 15% advantage is a good rule of thumb. By comparing the scores of your two top dogs it's easy to determine if a large enough difference exists.

Dog	Score
5	100
2	95
7	88
8	81
1	75
3	70
4	55
6	30

In the example above, only a 5% difference exists between the scores of the top two dogs, which makes a win bet impossible. Next is a second group of scores in a different race that suggests a win bet on the top animal.

Betting

Dog	Score
1	100
8	82
3	80
4	78
6	62
5	58
2	51
7	46

If a large enough score difference exists between the top two animals, betting to win is usually the best strategy. An exception would be very small tracks.

The problem with win bets at smaller tracks is that they affect the odds so dramatically. This happens because there is very little money in the betting pool to absorb the bet. A win bet as small as $100 on a dog that is a good play at 3-1 could drop it to even money, or worse.

Another problem encountered at tracks with a low handle is when two dogs are capable of winning a race and a player bets to win on the one with the best odds. After the bet, the odds on that dog immediately drop. This raises the odds on the second dog, the one that initially had the lower of the two odds. The second dog usually ends up winning the race at good odds and the player is left holding a losing ticket.

1-5	$2.40	5-2	$7.00	10-1	$22.00
2-5	2.80	3-1	8.00	15-1	32.00
3-5	3.20	7-2	9.00	20-1	42.00
4-5	3.60	4-1	10.00	25-1	52.00
1-1	4.00	9-2	11.00	30-1	62.00
6-5	4.40	5-1	12.00	40-1	82.00
7-5	4.80	6-1	14.00	50-1	102.00
8-5	5.20	7-1	16.00	60-1	122.00
9-5	5.60	8-1	18.00	70-1	142.00
2-1	6.00	9-1	20.00	80-1	162.00

Figure 10.1 - Odds and Payoffs for a $2 Bet

The chart above illustrates the actual payout of $2 bets at different odds. If you have a standout animal after you have handicapped the race, and are at a larger track, a win bet still makes a lot of sense.

Betting to Place

Some handicappers bet to place because they are not comfortable with betting to win. They feel that second place money is better than no money at all. There are reasons to bet place but that is not a very good one. But, if the odds and conditions are right, a place bet can be very profitable.

You should never bet a favorite at even money or less to place. This is because you are actually smarter to bet the animal to show. The payoff will probably be about the same and show gives you a little more breathing room if something goes wrong.

Example of a Place and
Show Payoff on a Favorite

<u>Win</u>	<u>Place</u>	<u>Show</u>
$3.80	3.20	3.20

An excellent place bet is if you have a strong contender that is 5-1 or better.

Dog	Score	Odds
5	100	2-1
2	95	6-1
7	88	3-1
8	81	10-1
1	75	8-1
3	70	15-1
4	55	9-2
6	30	22-1

Dog **#2** is an excellent place bet. If the favorite finishes out of the money, a place ticket will pay almost as much as the win.

Betting to Show

Some players have even less faith in their handicapping skills and are relegated to betting show. There is nothing wrong with show betting, except that you never reap a consistent profit, you merely lose slower while still cashing tickets.

Any contender that is worth betting to show is worth betting to win or place. If you feel the best dog can only be counted on to run third, then don't bet it at all, regardless of odds. An exception would be the following "two dog" strategy that consistently makes a profit.

Dog	Score	Odds
6	100	1-1
1	95	5-1
7	78	4-1
4	71	11-1
3	65	18-1
2	50	9-1
5	55	8-1
8	54	21-1

If you want both the favorite and a 5-1 (or better) odds dog to win a race, you can bet to show with a clear conscience. Contrary to what you are probably thinking, you actually bet the favorite to show and the long shot to win.

#1 to Win
 # 6 to Show

If the long shot (#1) wins, you will score big and probably still cash the show ticket on the favorite. If the favorite finishes in the top three, and the long shot runs out of the money, the show ticket will normally cover both bets. Try this strategy, it works!

Money Management for Straight Bets
The cardinal rule in wagering is that you always bet exactly the same on each race. This can either be a percentage of your bankroll or a fixed amount. Professional handicappers typically use the percentage sys-

tem, because when they win, they win more, and when they lose, they lose less.

As an illustration, let's look at two starting balances of $1000 and see which style works best. We'll begin by analyzing a four bet winning streak using 5% of $1000. (This is an example only, and does not mean you would bet this much.)

Using 5% of bankroll		
Bet	**Win/loss**	**Balance**
#1	$50 Win	$1050
#2	$52 Win	$1102
#3	$55 Win	$1157
#4	$58 Win	$1215
	Earnings	$215

Next we'll bet $50 on each race.

Straight Win bets		
Bet	**Win/loss**	**Balance**
#1	$50 Win	$1050
#2	$50 Win	$1100
#3	$50 Win	$1150
#4	$50 Win	$1200
	Earnings	$200

As you can see, by betting a percentage rather than a fixed amount of the bankroll, 7.5% more profit is realized. In our second example let's again start with $1000, but *lose* four races in a row.

Using 5% of Bankroll		
Bet	**Win/loss**	**Balance**
#1	$50 Loss	$950
#2	$47 Loss	$903
#3	$45 Loss	$858
#4	$43 Loss	$815
Total Loss		$185

Straight Win Bets		
Bet	**Win/loss**	**Balance**
#1	$50 Loss	$950
#2	$50 Loss	$900
#3	$50 Loss	$850
#4	$50 Loss	$800
Total Loss		$200

Again, using a percentage of the bankroll rather than a fixed amount, losses were reduced by 7.5%.

Either of these methods are still better than increasing or decreasing the amount of your wager on each race. If you fail to bet consistently, I guarantee that you will win the $5 and lose the $50 bets. Always bet the same increment, and do not fall in love with a dog or a race.

Understanding the Trifecta
The most popular bet at any dog track is the **Trifecta**. Over 50% of all the money bet each day is on the

Trifecta, so this is definitely where the action is. To win, you must pick the top three finishers in exact order of finish. There are other exotic bets, but the Trifecta is the most heavily played, has the best payoffs and is the one we will focus on.

As opposed to straight bets, payoffs in the Trifecta can't be determined by the dog's actual odds at post. With eight dogs there are 336 possible Trifecta combinations, and only one is a winner.

If the top three favorites finish 1, 2, and 3, the Trifecta payoff will obviously be smaller than if three long shots cross the finish line. This is about as close as you can come to approximating how much a ticket is worth in these types of bets.

Illogical Betting Techniques

I have been at the track when the three favorites finished 1-2-3 and the Trifecta payoff was higher than the next race when a 10-1 long shot won. This defies logic, but let's examine how some of the crowd's betting techniques can cause it to happen.

Low paying Trifectas that include long shots often occur because of the winning dog's number or the numbers of all three finishers. An example would be a long shot running from the 7 box. Number 7 dogs are often **bet down**, overplayed, regardless of their ability because they are considered "lucky" by many bettors.

Others prefer colors and often box the red, white and blue. It is patriotic, but not very logical. Low payoffs in maiden or other unbeatable races attest to the fact that players make illogical bets.

By playing the actual contenders, you will cash many more tickets than players who rely on lucky numbers or colors. You will also get better than expected payoffs because the "stupid money" is part of the betting pool and smart players usually take it.

Trifecta Strategy
The first Trifecta strategy is to make the optimum number of bets on each race. Winning with a single bet is almost impossible because handicapping is not an exact science and you can only approximate the finish. Betting a huge box or wheel in order to "buy a race" also isn't productive. Huge bets are normally an excuse for sloppy handicapping, plus the cost of the ticket is usually higher than the payoff.

In order to make your bet manageable, first identify the contenders and then determine if any of them are standouts. If a contender has a combined score at least 15% higher than any other contender in the race, it is a **standout**, and you will be able to bet a wheel. If you do not have a standout, you must bet a box. Let's first look at the easier box bet.

Boxing Dogs in Trifecta

The simplest type of Trifecta bet is to box all of the dogs that you feel have a chance to finish in the top three positions. When using this method it is essential to throw out as many non-contenders as possible because the costs rise considerably with each dog.

Figure 10.2 shows the cost per box based on how many dogs are included. For $336 you can box all eight dogs in the $1 Trifecta and be guaranteed a winner, but you will probably lose money.

Total Number of Dogs	Trifecta Box	Number of Bets	$1.00 Base Bet Total Cost	$2.00 Base Bet Total Cost
3	Dog Box	6	$ 6.00	$ 12.00
4	Dog Box	24	24.00	48.00
5	Dog Box	60	60.00	120.00
6	Dog Box	120	120.00	240.00
7	Dog Box	210	210.00	420.00
8	Dog Box	336	336.00	672.00

Figure 10.2 - Trifecta Box

Let's assume that after handicapping a race, five dogs stand out as the best in the race and you feel that no other dog should be in the top three.

The first thing to do is to look for a standout. According to the scores there is no standout, because dog **#1** (the top dog) is only 8 points higher than the second dog (dog **#3**) and this is less than 15%. The second step is to figure out which dogs can be thrown out, and the 15% rule works there also. Dog **#2** is more than 15% lower than dog **#7**, so all dogs below dog **#7** are dropped from the bet.

Dog	Score
1	100
3	92
4	87
6	80
7	**76**
2	58
8	51
5	46

The contenders are now boxed in the Trifecta. Three of the five dogs must finish in the top three in order for you to cash the ticket, and the cost is $60.

Five Contenders in your race: **1, 3, 4, 6, 7**

Cost = $60 for $1.00 Trifecta Box.

It is imperative that you throw at least three dogs out of each Trifecta box, otherwise the cost of the box doesn't justify the possible payoff. This is especially true if your box includes all of the favorites.

Using a Limited Wheel
The most powerful and least expensive Trifecta bet is the **limited wheel**. There are two things necessary to create a limited wheel, the first is a key dog and the second is a reduced number of contenders. In the last

section the field was reduced to five contenders, but since there was no key dog, a Trifecta box bet was necessary.

Finding the Key Dog

When playing a limited wheel, the **key dog** must finish first or second in order for you to win the Trifecta. That means it must have at least a 15% advantage over the second best contender. In the example below, dog **#8** qualifies as a key dog because it is 18 points higher than Dog **#5**.

Dog	Score
8	**100**
5	82
4	80
7	72
6	70
1	65
3	50
2	40

It doesn't matter if the key dog is a favorite or a long shot, it just must outclass the field enough to easily win the race, or at worst come in second. Remember, if a race does not include a key dog you must either pass the race or box all of the contenders.

Eliminating Non-Contenders

You must always try to eliminate as many of the dogs as possible so the bet will not be too expensive. But, only non-contenders can be eliminated from a wheel. If you throw out any contenders, to save money or for any other reason, wheeling (or boxing, for that matter) becomes very risky and is not very good strategy.

The easiest way to decide which dogs are the contenders is to study the scores. You already know that a key dog must always be at least 15% or 15 points higher than the second highest dog, or there is no key dog. The next break between dogs that is equal to or larger than 15 points separates the **contenders**, forcing all dogs below it to be eliminated from the bet.

In the following example, dog #6 is the key with dogs 1, 3, 4 and 7, the contenders. The 16 point difference between dog #7 and dog #2 forces dogs 2, 5 and 8 to be thrown out of the wheel.

Dog	Score
6	100
1	72
3	67
4	60
7	60
2	44
5	41
8	36

With a key dog, and hopefully four (or less) contenders, you will be able to cash a very respectable percentage of Trifecta tickets.

Number of Contenders

If you wheel all seven remaining dogs with your key dog this is not considered a limited wheel because you didn't limit the number of possible dogs. It is also another sign of poor handicapping similar to boxing eight dogs.

The highest number of contenders that you should wheel with your key dog is five. This increases the bet to $20 for each wheel, but if there are five true contenders it still makes sense. Figure 10.3 illustrates the cost for each wheel.

Total Number of Dogs	Trifecta Box	Contenders	Number of Bets	$1.00 Base Bet Total Cost	$2.00 Base Bet Total Cost
4	Key Dog	3	6	$ 6.00	$12.00
5	Key Dog	4	12	12.00	24.00
6	Key Dog	5	20	20.00	40.00
7	Key Dog	6	30	30.00	60.00
8	Key Dog	7	42	42.00	84.00

Figure 10.3 - Key Entry Chart

Earlier it was noted that an 8 dog box in the $1 Trifecta cost $336. Wheeling the field with a key dog reduces that amount to only $42.

Creating a Limited Wheel

By creating a limited wheel you get the most amount of coverage for the least amount of money. Below is an example using the same contenders that were boxed earlier. The only difference is that dog #6 is the key dog.

Highest rated dog in the race.	6
Top 4 contenders.	1, 3, 4, 7
Limited wheel, key dog win position only.	6 (win)
	____
	1, 3, 4, 7 (place)
	____
	1, 3, 4, 7 (show)

The **#6** is the key dog and is positioned on top with the four contenders. It must win the race, but any combination of contenders can finish second or third and the example above illustrates what the wheel and your betting ticket would look like. This bet costs $12.00 and wins 1/2 of the $2.00 Trifecta. This is a lot less expensive than the $60 that was required earlier to box all five dogs.

Limited Wheel In Both Positions

Because of the possible running problems in a race, I suggest that you wheel the key dog in both the first and second finishing positions. You will win a much larger percentage of Trifecta's using this method. On the followin page is what your expanded limited wheel should look like.

Highest rated dog in the race.	6	
Top 4 contenders.	1, 3, 4, 7	
Limited wheel, win and place position.	6	1, 3, 4, 7 (win)
	<u>1, 3, 4, 7</u> <u>6</u>	(place)
	<u>1, 3, 4, 7</u> <u>1, 3, 4, 7</u>	(show)

Dog **#6** can now finish first or second, with any contender in the remaining positions, and the ticket is a winner. This $1.00 Trifecta Limited Wheel costs $24, but is the most effective bet possible and is still $36 cheaper than a five dog box.

It is not productive to continue this progression by placing the key dog third (with the contenders first and second). After extensive testing, the key dog finished third just enough times to pay the extra $12 necessary to place the bet. Key dogs that failed to finish first or second have a tendency to run out of the money.

Money Management and Exotic Bets
When you are playing exotics you must bet the same increment on each playable race. You may have to include more contenders, raising the cost of the wheel, but you never alternate between the $1.00 and the $2.00 Trifecta. A race should not be bet unless it is playable, and no playable race is any better than another, so keep your increments equal.

After your bankroll is larger, it is perfectly acceptable to increase your wheels from $1.00 to $2.00 or even $5.00, but not on the same race day. Always spread your bets evenly over the day's playable races so your wins and losses average out into a profit. Remember, races are either playable or they are not, there is no middle ground.

Increasing Your Profit Expectation

For those players serious about winning and looking to get the maximum advantage at the track, I strongly recommend the professional level strategiy in the back.

GLOSSARY

1/8th Call—The position of a greyhound at the second call or 1/8th mile mark in a race.

Actual Running Time—A greyhound's individual finish time in a race.

Average Early Speed—The averaged ability of a greyhound to perform best in the earlier parts of a race. The Average Early Speed is calculated by adding the start calls from a greyhound's last 6 races and dividing them by 6. The lower the number the better the score.

Average Speed—Average amount of time in seconds it takes a greyhound to complete a race relative to the track record. The Average Speed Score is calculated by adding the last three finish times, dividing them by three, subtracting the average from the track record and multiplying by ten. A zero is the best score possible.

Back Runner—A Running Style where a greyhound tends to race behind the rest of the pack.

Bankroll—The amount of money set aside or designated for a day's worth of betting.

Box Bias—A starting position that exhibits a distinct advantage or disadvantage in win percentage.

Box Position—A greyhound's starting point in the race. There are normally 8 positions starting with Box 1 on the inside of the track, and finishing with Box 8 on the outside. The most favorable box position is dependent on the greyhound's running style.

Breakage—The difference between the actual money in the betting pool and the final payout to the winners. With favorites, this percentage can be substantial.

Break Call—The call made just as the greyhounds leave the starting box.

Class—See Effective Grade.

Closing Ability—The ability of a greyhound to perform best in the latter parts of a race. Closing Ability is calculated by adding the 1/8th call from a greyhound's last six races, dividing them by six, and subtracting this average from the average of the last six finish calls.

Comments—A description of a greyhound's performance in a particular race.

Contender—A greyhound that is considered a favorite to finish in the top three positions of a race.

Daily Double—A wager that requires picking the winner of the first and second races.

Distance—The length of a race noted in fractions of a mile or feet (3/16, 3/8, 5/16, 5/8 or 990, 1980, 1650, 3300).

Early Speed—The ability of a greyhound to perform best in the earlier parts of a race.

Effective Grade—The grade which reflects a greyhound's current running ability, regardless of current grade designation. Also referred to as Class.

Effective Grade Score—Numeric designation for a greyhound's Effective Grade, calculated by adding grade point designations for races with a 3rd place or better finish position, and dividing by the number of races used.

Exotic Bet—A wager, such as a Trifecta.

Glossary

Final Call—See Finish Call.

Finish Call—The position of a greyhound at the end of a race.

Form—A greyhound's running ability at any given period in time.

Front Runner—Running Style where a greyhound tends to race in the front of the pack.

Grade—An alphabetic identification system used to classify the quality of a greyhound or race. (i.e. A, B, C, D, E, M)

Grade Point Score—Numeric classification of Grade used to calculate each greyhound's Effective Grade. (A=5, B=4, C=3, D=2, E=1)

Inside Runner—Running Style where a greyhound tends to race toward the rail or the inside of the track.

Kennel—The name of the individual or entity responsible for the caretaking of a greyhound.

Kennel Rating—A numeric classification denoting kennel quality.

Key Dog—A contender greyhound with at least a 15 percent or 15 point total score advantage over the second best greyhound.

Limited Wheel—A betting technique using a reduced rotation system to produce combinations of a "Key Dog" and contenders.

Maiden—A greyhound that has not yet won a race in any grade. Also the name for a type or grade of race.

Odds—A betting term that defines each greyhound's potential payoff in a race.

Outside Runner—Running Style where a greyhound tends to race toward the outside of the track.

Place Bet—Wagering that a greyhound of your choice will finish either first or second.

Program—Official track listing of each race, the greyhounds in each race with their past performance data, race results, and other helpful information such as betting tips & track rules.

Recent Form—A greyhound's running performance in its most recent races. The three terms used to define a greyhound's *Recent Form* are **Positive**, **Neutral**, and **Negative**.

Relative Grade—A shipper's grade relative to the grade at the track where he will be running. The grade that corresponds to your local grade for shippers.

Running Style—The specific characteristics that describe the manner in which a greyhound runs a race.

Schooling Race—A type of race with no grade classification, where greyhounds run only to prepare for future graded races.

Second Call—The call made 1/8 of a mile after start call and is at different points on the track depending on which course is run.

Shipper—A greyhound whose previous race was run at a different track.

Show Bet—Wagering that a greyhound of your choice will finish either first, second, or third.

Speed—The amount of time in seconds it takes a greyhound to complete a race relative to the track record.

Start Call—The position of a greyhound at the start of a race after coming out of the box, or first call.

Straight Bet—A wager, such as a Win, Place, or Show.

Stretch Call—The position of a greyhound at the straight-away before the finish of a race, or third call.

Trifecta—A wager that requires picking the first three finishers of a race in exact order.

Tote Board—A display board at a track that lists each greyhound's current odds.

Track—The name or abbreviation of a greyhound course where races are run.

Track Condition—A description of the track's running surface during a given race. The Track Condition is listed on the racing program as a one letter abbreviation; F - Fast, M - Muddy, S - Slow.

Track Rating—A numeric designation for identifying the quality of a track. (5 Excellent, 4 Good, 3 Average, 2 Sub-Standard, 1 Poor)

Track Take—The money kept by the track out of the betting pool to pay its expenses.

Weight—A greyhound's race weight in pounds, one hour prior to the start of the race.

Wheel—A betting technique using a rotation system to produce all possible combinations of a key greyhound and all other greyhounds in a race.

Win Bet—Wagering that a greyhound of your choice will finish first in a race.

Win Percentage—The number of Win, Place or Show finishes divided by the total number of finishes.

Winner's Time—The winning greyhound's individual finish time in a race.

GREYHOUND LEVEL V™

Prof. Jones Winning Software - For Professional Players
IBM & Compatibles Only - Hard Drive Required

• THE ULTIMATE WINNING PACKAGE!!! •

Groups of questions can be assigned to create your own scores and comparison charts. For example, if you feel 1/8 to final call is "Closing Ability", you can apply only this variable; or you can add lengths gained or lost from stretch to finish.

You truly create your own program from the ground up.

ASSIGN GROUPS			
GROUP	LOW	HIGH	STATUS
EARLY SPEED	0	1	OFF
CLOSING ABILITY	-10	10	ON
GRADE CHANGE	-6	10	ON
BOX	0	5	ON
CLASS	-8	20	ON
PACE	-1	13	OFF
KENNEL	04	12	ON
OV. SPEED	-1	4	ON
STYLE	0	5	ON
STARTS	0	3	ON
TRACK LAST	0	2	ON
FINISH LAST	-5	6	ON
1/8 LAST	-4	8	OFF
DIST PREV	-6	9	ON
1ST	-0	1	ON
2NDS	02	12	ON

Level V allows Linear Multiple Regression (Artifical Intelligence) to be applied to both your STANDARD VALUES and DATABASE VALUES. The more you run the program, the higher your win percentage will be.

Artifical intelligence will even tell you if your weighting systems are correct or if they should be changed. You can now create "perfect" weights.

	USING STANDARD SCORES		
NAME	PROJ	MUs	COMPARISONS
4-ACCLAIMED	1-4	-	1-Concensus
7-MY KIM	5-1	3	3-Grade, 1-Class, 3-Early SP
1-GOIN FOR DOUGH	5-1	↓	1-Pace, 3-Close
5-KING SWEETY	7-1	2	2-Concensus
9-PLEASE	8-1	1	3-Concensus

- NO MOVE UP
↓ MOVED DOWN
MOVED UP # OF PLACES

NAME	MOVE-UPS
7-MY KIM	3
5-KING SWEETY	2
9-PLEASE	1

Move ups compare standard and any other set of results.

Top 3 in each catagory taken directly from the comparison chart.

Using Standard Scores	
NAME	POINTS
7-MY KIM	16
9-PLEASE	15
5-KING SWEETY	13
1-GOIN FOR DOUGH	2

'Top Overlays' compares morning line odds and the projected odds.

New advanced betting analysis allows you to program **all** forms of bets. Complete odds projections are given for each animal and all 'overlays' are displayed.

TRIFECTA	
7	1-4-5-9
1-4-5-9	7
1-4-5-9	1-4-5-9

4-ACCLAIMED 7-MY KIM
1-GOIN FOR DOUGH 5-KING SWEETY
9-PLEASE

COST IS 24 UNITS

07/03/1990 BOI											RACE NUMBER	
BET TYPE	1	2	3	4	5	6	7	8	9	0	1	Control Keys
Win/Place/Show												↑ Cursor Up X Selected
Top 2 Any Order	X											↓ Cursor Down
Top 2 Any Order												→ Cursor Right ◆ Cursor
Top 3 Any Order	X											← Cursor Left
Top 4 Any Order	◆											C -Clear All ■ Can't Bet

R -Select All bets for a race
V -View a Bet
<ESC> Exit

The advanced 'Dog Watch List' links directly to the enter section so animals in trouble last out are flagged instantly.

Race 01	Post 01
Race 02	Post 02
Race 03	Post 03
Race 04	Post 04
Race 05	Post 05
Race 06	Post 06
Race 07	Post 07
Race 08	Post 08
Race 09	Post 09

DISTANCE: 5/16   WEIGHTING: A LONG   RACE DATE: 06/18/90
DOG'S NAME: MY KIM

WATCH LIST

ENTRY DATE: 06/02/90
MESSAGE:
BUMPED IN FIRST TURN
BUT RECOVERED WELL

PRESS ANY KEY

Create your own Greyhound racing program for your track with the first "User Programmable" handicapping product.

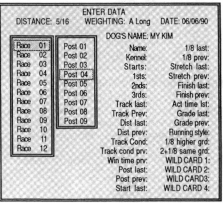